THE JUST KITCHEN

INVITATIONS TO SUSTAINABILITY, COOKING, CONNECTION, AND CELEBRATION

DERRICK WESTON & ANNA WOOFENDEN

Broadleaf Books
Minneapolis

THE JUST KITCHEN

Invitations to Sustainability, Cooking, Connection, and Celebration

Library of Congress Control Number 2023008897 (print)

Cover design: 1517 Media
Cover image: GettyImages/DigitalVision Vectors; Pumpkin Pie Illustration by askmenow
Interior images: The Noun Project, www.thenounproject.com (microphone, leaf, fish); Vecteezy.com (all other kitchen utensils)

Print ISBN: 978-1-5064-8411-2
eBook ISBN: 978-1-5064-8412-9

Printed in China

For my mother and grandmothers, who nurtured me in their kitchens.
For my spouse David, it is a gift to share our kitchen and life with you.
And for our daughter, Jarena, who is showing us the way.
—Anna

For Sophia, Gus, Thomas, Maggie, and Shannon, my favorite reasons to be
in the kitchen. And for my grandfather, Thomas Boling, who claimed
that he invented the grilled cheese.
—Derrick

CONTENTS

Introduction: Reimagining Our Kitchens

There are a lot of books about food. Walk into your local bookstore, and you will find food histories, anthropological studies of food, scientific studies of what you should eat and why, and of course, any number of diet books and cookbooks. We—Derrick and Anna—have read a lot of these books. And as the cohosts (along with our friend Sam Chamelin) of *The Food and Faith Podcast*, we often get to speak with the chefs, writers, and activists who wrote them. But as we surveyed the landscape of what is written about food, we began to notice something missing.

There's an important, growing number of books about the brokenness of the food system, particularly the extractive ways most of our food is produced. Other books focus on eating, usually highlighting the joys and benefits of slowing down and eating together in community. But what we only rarely saw were books focusing on where much of our time is actually spent: between food being produced and food being served, between the corn growing in the field and the grilled corn hitting the table. There's just not much written about the kitchen and cooking itself, particularly from the lens of faith and justice. Oh, there are a lot of cookbooks, but there aren't a lot of books *about* cooking.

We want to have this book in the world because what happens in our kitchens takes a significant amount of our time, resources, and energy. We want to talk about these things because, whether we recognize it or not, we put a lot of who we are and much of what we value into our cooking. And we believe that what happens in our kitchens matters.

We are not chefs. We are not food scholars. We are not culinary historians. We are two people who love talking about food and the spiritual connection to it, and we are two people who are committed to asking questions. During the run of *The*

Food and Faith Podcast, we have asked our guests and ourselves questions you may have as well, such as:

- Where does the food we bring into our kitchens come from?

- Is it equitably accessed? If so, how? Could it be sourced more equitably?

- How does that food and how we prepare it help form community at the table?

More than one hundred guests from across the human spectrum have shared their stories with us and with listeners, allowing us to glimpse their lives and kitchen stories in how they speak to the intersection of food and faith in their own experience.

In the following pages, we bring some of those stories and questions to our kitchens and yours—that same interrogative lens and attention to lived experience—as we contemplate what happens in our kitchen spaces. We asked our friends, interviewees, and colleagues who care about food and about doing good in the world what is happening in their kitchens. We talked to professionals in the food industry—but not many, because we want to keep the focus on what "real people" are doing to bring their values into their homes. We talked to historians and people who know about the larger food system, to bring a sense of context. But mostly we talked to people who like to cook and who spend a lot of time in their kitchen. We also talked to a few people who *don't* like to cook but have to anyway, to learn valuable insights about time constraints and busy households and how all of that relates to their kitchens. We asked:

- How does food shape you?

- Who in your household does the cooking, and why?

- What has influenced decisions around what foods you choose to cook and serve?

- In what ways is your personal history reflected in food and in food preparation?

- In what ways have larger historical or cultural forces influenced what you cook in your home?

What we discovered and what we share here is that our kitchens hold a lot more than food.

OUR HOPES FOR THIS BOOK

You are going to see the word "hope" frequently throughout this book. Hope, we believe, is an important element of justice. Hope is the ability to imagine a better world, one where wrongs are made right, where those bent low by the world are lifted up, and where everyone has what they need to not only live but thrive. When we talk about hope, we're not talking about a naive wishing that ignores the problems of the world. We are talking about a resiliency that gets us out of bed in the morning despite the world's challenges. Each chapter ends with someone we've introduced giving a glimpse of what gives them hope. May their reflections give you a moment to ponder where you find hope as well.

In the final chapter, the two of us will share what gives us hope personally, but we start here with our hopes *for this book*. We hope it will live in your kitchen alongside your cookbooks. We hope it will be a resource you reference both for the practical tips and recipes and as you revisit the reflections when your own kitchen feels far from ideal. For some of you, this book will reinforce the good work you've begun and offer encouragement to go the next few steps. For others of you, we hope this book improves your relationship with your kitchen. For still others, we hope this book will be the catalyst to start that relationship. We hope this book influences your feelings about food and its power to connect us. We hope we all can begin seeing our kitchens as sacred places where important things happen, and not just as another room where menial tasks are performed. Finally, we hope you'll recognize that it doesn't take a lot to make a just kitchen: it requires willingness to see your place in an interconnected world, intention to do your part even if all you can do is something small, and deep belief that when many of us do what we can, where we can, as often as we can, we will in fact help heal our world.

One final note: Our drive for just kitchens is deeply rooted in our faith. We're both grounded in the Christian tradition, which is something of a native tongue for us. That said, just kitchens don't have to be Christian, Jewish, Muslim, or representative of any faith tradition. Just kitchens can be in homes of any faith or no faith at all. At times in this book, we use specifically Christian language, but we do so to illustrate truths we believe are also universal. We invite you to consider how those ideas translate for you.

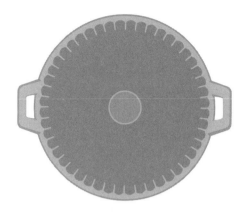

CHAPTER 1

THE KITCHEN AS A KEEPER OF STORY AND HISTORY

There's something about the kitchen that both draws us in and repels us. Many people, including us, consider the kitchen the center of their home. When people visit, we find they tend to congregate there. When someone is cooking, all the kids and adults gather; even the pets can be found underfoot. The kitchen is often called "the heart of the home"; there is a magnetic force about the kitchen that draws everyone in.

In contrast, we noticed throughout our interviews that guest after guest, when asked about their experiences in their kitchen, quickly wandered to thoughts about the dining table or fast-forwarded to the eating of the meal. As we read through the interview transcripts, we repeatedly found ourselves nudging guests to return to the process of food preparation with such lines as "Interesting . . . now can I draw you *back into the kitchen* for this question?" Or "I love how you describe being at the table, but can you tell us about how that shows up *in the kitchen*?"

As we kept experiencing the narrative of avoiding the kitchen, we wondered and asked why this was so common. Why is it easier to talk about the presentation and eating of a meal than the preparation of it? Why does the idea of sourcing ingredients and making family recipes bring excitement to people's voices, but the actual chopping and stirring calls forth resistance?

There's no one answer to these questions, but food preparation is the most "practical" and time-consuming part of the process, so we believe it's important to learn from the tensions we hold to see what we can discover. We feel these tensions too. And as we began unpacking our own resistance to the kitchen, a floodgate of stories and feelings opened up in us. We explored these stories as we cooked, and in the act of cooking with intention, with an eye toward justice, we found the hope to forge a new way of being in our kitchens as they were transformed into more just and faithful spaces.

A HISTORY OF POWER

Along with the stories of joyful gatherings with families and friends in the kitchen, there are other kitchen stories that are fraught. In much of Western history, and in our own stories, cooking involves an undeniable power dynamic. Whether that is women being expected to cook for men or enslaved people cooking for their enslavers, there has been a long history of cooking as the role of subservient ones.

While that power dynamic may not be as pronounced in the modern kitchen as it was in the past, we still feel its influence. According to a 2019 Pew Research study, women remain the primary shoppers and cooks in the average household, even when both partners work. In homes where one partner works outside the home and the other does not—even if that one *works for pay from* home—the seeming expectation is that the one at home should cook *for* the one who goes off to work. The power dynamic is also reflected in who we see working in restaurant, hotel, school, and other kitchens across our country. It's often work left for people of color, recent or undocumented immigrants, and others we generally term "unskilled." Anthony Bourdain gives a "commencement speech" in the conclusion of his classic memoir *Kitchen Confidential: Adventures in the Culinary Underbelly*. In it he tells would-be chefs, "Much of the workforce in the industry you are about to enter is Spanish-speaking. The very backbone of the industry, whether you like it or not, is inexpensive Mexican, Dominican, Salvadorian, and Ecuadorian labor—most of whom could cook you under the table without breaking a sweat."

Acknowledging this historical power dynamic may be the beginning of rethinking the ways we tend to one another and of changing our perception of cooking from a menial task to a loving act of service—not just in *our* kitchens, but in *all* kitchens in our cultures. It can be the beginning of turning meal preparation from a chore to a ritual, from an obligation to an offering. As we recognize that the kitchen has long been a place of bondage, we can begin to reimagine it as a place of liberation and justice. Though the kitchen has often been a place where people work mechanically, it holds potential to be a place where people move creatively. In many ways, the first call to a just kitchen is the call to decolonize the idea of what the kitchen is. When we reimagine the kitchen as less a place where subordinates are relegated, and more a place where equals share mutuality, we bring ourselves and others into just kitchens. The just kitchen begins with deemphasizing expediency and efficiency and shifting to something very different: savoring the time to reflect, heal, and be transformed.

IDEAL vs. REAL

In our homes, we often meet pressure and expectations to feed our families, but to do so in a way that is ethically and environmentally sound, well balanced, and nutritious. We realize that so much of what we explore in this book—such as how we source our food and cook with intention—can be both an inspiration and a burden. For us, sometimes preparing food is one more thing we're failing at three times a day. Can you relate?

In our conversations, we heard even more: the shared experience of not having enough time to cook or enough time to cook in the way we'd like. And all the "shoulds" and expectations—if we only managed our time better, we'd have time to cook. There were also stories of not having the financial resources to cook as we'd like. We met the reality of living in the late-stage capitalism that Emily and Amelia Nagoski describe in their book *Burnout: Solve Your Stress Cycle*: the sense that "the system is rigged." It's actually not possible for a two-person, two-job household, let alone a one-parent one, to work, run the household, potentially take care of children, *and* cook three meals a day, seven days a week, in the way we'd like to cook—because, at the end of the day, cooking is about time and labor.

Many of us have an idealized history of kitchens. We might picture the 1950s *Leave It to Beaver* kitchen. What do we find there? One of the adults—the female, of course—with cooking and cleaning as her main role. That's how she spent her days. Or in many middle- and upper-income households, resources were available to hire people—usually people of color and people of lesser economic means—to do the cooking and cleaning. Rewinding further back through history brings to mind other idealized meals we've envisioned: from the pioneer farmers' Sunday dinners with tables laden with dishes the women worked on all day, to the feasts depicted on plantations and estates. All of these scenes have some kind of labor behind them. Whether it was the toil of the women of the family, the hired help, or enslaved people, for a household kitchen to produce three meals a day, seven days a week, it took people—often quite a few people—who were primarily dedicated to cooking.

And multiple people primarily dedicated to cooking is not the reality most of us live in. No wonder we avoid the kitchen! It's loaded with a history of oppressive labor, and with expectations of how it could be, or should be—without the resources, personnel, and energy to fulfill that vision.

Before we go any further, we want to explicitly echo the words "the system is rigged." We can't actually do it all and have it all, all the time. It is unreasonable to think that every meal we eat can be made with the level of intention and care we would like. It's unreasonable to believe we all can and will source everything we eat in the ethically and environmentally sustainable way we might want. Even as we decry the plastic food wrappings in our trash can and, yet again, put rotten produce into the compost (telling ourselves, *At least we compost!*), the truth is, having a just kitchen is a high ideal and not always perfectly possible.

But there is hope—the kind of hope that doesn't ignore the difficult things, but that looks them in the eye and moves toward transformation and liberation. We believe the kitchen truly can be a place of transformation and liberation, of celebration and healing, of reflection and community—a place of hope.

In the faith tradition of which we're both a part, one of our central sacraments is a meal. Some in the Christian tradition call it "communion"; others, "Eucharist" (from the Greek, meaning "thanksgiving"); and others, "the Lord's Supper." Whatever it is called, it rises from a time when Jesus gathered with a motley crew of followers and friends to share a meal together. At this meal, the night before he was crucified, Jesus took bread, blessed it, broke it, and told his followers that eating that bread was an act of remembrance. Later on during the meal, he took a cup of wine, blessed it, and shared it, proclaiming that it was to be imbibed in remembrance of him. This sacrament, so central to many, is simply coming around a table and eating together.

As we might say to a podcast guest, "I see we went straight to the table. Can we draw our focus back to the preparation?" Yes, to those who sourced the elements and set the table, but also to that which comes before the sacred meal in many traditions' liturgies: the review of conscience, what some call the confession—a time to ponder the habits and thoughts that separate us from our ground of faith and one another. This time before the sacred meal allows us to reflect on what blocks us from the ever-present and life-giving love of the Divine and the reciprocal love we're called to have for one another.

We mention this because, as with communion, while your typical meal at home includes preparation—cutting, heating, stirring—the time before the meal might also be an invitation to ponder: *What separates us from the ground of all being? From our community? Our neighbors? What is separating us from feeling we are fully beloved children of God?* Yes, we ask such questions during religious services before partaking of a shared sacred meal, but what if we asked ourselves, as the soup's reheating, *How do our interactions in the kitchen and our stories around the kitchen separate us from one another? In what ways are our kitchens not just?* Because at their core, the unjust power dynamics we've described are about separation from one another. Asking ourselves how we participate in that separation is a good initial step.

As a way to grow into community and justice, we want to explore these questions with you and talk about what makes for a just kitchen. But before we do that, it might be helpful for you to get to know our geographies as authors, specifically those geographies that relate directly to the kitchen and the way it has shaped our view of the world. Throughout this book you'll find similar sidebars. We hope these will make ideas for a just kitchen personal and specific, to help you see how your own story affects your kitchen and table as well.

My Evolving Kitchen
Anna's Story

I was around eight years old, sitting on the threadbare couch in the living room of our partially finished, small wooden house in northwest Washington. Looking across toward the kitchen stove, I saw my mom standing there, stirring. One younger sibling was setting up wooden train tracks around the kitchen table legs. Another, just proficient at crawling, traversed the floor, often getting under my mom's feet as she cooked. Occasionally, a pan lid clanked more loudly than necessary as a frustration and exhaustion I didn't understand at the time boiled in my mother.

By the time dinner was on the table, her mood was often marked by weariness. The fact that most every night of my childhood there was a full and well-balanced, healthy, and often locally sourced meal on the table for our large family by 6:30 p.m. is not the texture of the memory (though it's now something I deeply appreciate and honor). Instead, it's the tired look in my mother's eyes, my father's attempt to make dinnertime conversation, and the sense that meal-times were "supposed" to be something more joyful than they often were.

It wasn't until I left home for college and started spending time in other kitchens that I could articulate and reflect on the tension I felt between whether the kitchen was a place of joy and warmth or a place of depletion and exhaustion. While living with a family in Colorado during an internship in college, I experienced the kitchen as a more consistently life-giving place. And in this case it wasn't the mother of the family doing the cooking either. Dave is a fantastic cook, and it seemed to bring him joy to look through the fridge when he got home from work and start chopping and putting things together. I quickly found that the kitchen table was the place to be in this house, with two little kids running around, grown-ups chatting, and good food being made. My childhood assumptions about whose responsibility it was to feed the family were broken wide open: it turns out that the person who loves cooking and is good at it should be the one who cooks, rather than traditional gender roles dictating that. I began to reimagine what the kitchen could be in my life and the lives of others.

Food and Identity
Derrick's Story

When you are young, food is food. It never would have crossed my mind as a kid to think of "Black" foods and "white" foods, but as I got older, and got to peek into more of my suburban white friends' kitchens, it slowly dawned on me that what was happening in the kitchens of my youth was the preparation of Black food. Along with that realization came questions about the value of what was happening in my kitchen. Internalized racism asks, "If white people aren't doing it, does that make it inferior?" Such questions didn't linger, because what was coming out of the Black kitchens of my younger days was delicious! Though I ceased questioning the merit of the food itself, I was left with the observation that what was happening in our kitchen was a part of who we are, and that had value.

Over time, our family's kitchen would become more "white." Maybe a better way of saying that is that our kitchen became more middle-class American. More frozen things, more prepackaged things, more instant things. As time in the kitchen became more of a luxury for everyone in the house, convenience took precedence over culture. The casualty of this convenience was the loss of generational memory of what happens in Black kitchens. At some point, we lost sight of the kitchen as a place to preserve our culture. This, it seems, happens to a lot of us, regardless of race.

Though both my brother and I experimented and treasured our foods, our attempts to make fried chicken like our mom's ended in grease fires. We wouldn't have named it as such, but those failures were an attempt at keeping something of our past alive. I'm just now learning what to do with collard greens, thanks to the volumes on Black cooking. (I insist on growing them every year . . . for the ancestors.)

My early twenties were a blur of fast food. My late twenties and early thirties, though, were a time of slowly reintroducing myself to the kitchen space. I imagined myself a large-event chef, using as many pots and pans as possible to create elaborate meals (at least by my standards). That's also when I began to love cooking shows. And let's not forget the grill! I was thirty when I got my first grill. Grilling is an oddly gendered activity, an acceptable way to cook and still be manly. Though I've become suspicious of the gender dynamics that exist around cooking over fire, I still love grilling. And while the grill is outside, I consider it an extension of the kitchen.

Over the last decade, my cooking has been paired with an increased love of gardening, which has included an appreciation for African American contributions to the agriculture of this country. My interests now are around what cooking says about the people and cultures represented in the kitchen. I love shows like Chef's Table and Ugly Delicious, and anything with the late Anthony Bourdain. Cooking has become for me a way of getting to know people, their history, and their values. This includes my own heritage. Some foods represent struggle and oppression. Others represent resilience and ingenuity. Still others represent celebration and victory. And you can have all of those experiences represented on one plate!

WHAT DO YOU BRING TO YOUR KITCHEN?

The first kitchen counter I remember is _____ (color and material),
In my _____ (who's home) home.
_____ (person) is _____ (action) there,
Hands _____ (action of hands), and _____ (sound or words) coming
from _____ (pronoun) lips.

Our home was on the land of _____ (tree/plant) and _____ (animal),
_____ (geographic description),
Surrounded by _____ (geographic description).

I remember the _____ (ingredient) and _____ (ingredient),
_____ (cooking action) together to make _____ (dish).
The smell of _____ (food) mixing with _____ (another food smell),
Filling the room.

My _____ (important person in your life)
Cooked _____ (dish),
With _____ (action) and _____ (value).

Sometimes I was invited to _____ (an action in the kitchen),
And other times I _____ (another action in the kitchen).
And I always knew _____ (how it felt to be in that kitchen).

As I grew, I discovered that kitchens could also be _____ (description of other
    kitchens you experienced) and _____ (another description).
And I found _____ (feeling) in creating places of _____ (descriptor)
    and _____ (descriptor).

Today in my kitchen you'll find _____ (kitchen equipment),
On _____ (material of kitchen counter),
With _____ (kitchen equipment) standing by.

_____ (ingredient) and _____ (ingredient) _____ (action done
    to food)
To make _____ (dish).
_____ (sound) mingle with _____ (smell) as _____ (meal) is
    made.

While some days my kitchen is _____ (description),
There is always hope for _____ (description).
As I long to be part of creating a more _____ (value) and _____
    (value) world.

WHAT DO YOU BRING TO YOUR KITCHEN? (ANNA)

The first kitchen counter I remember is warm oak wood
In my parents' home.
My mother is cooking there,
Hands kneading the vat of bread dough, and singing coming from her lips.

Our home was on the land of Douglas fir trees and bald eagles,
A small island, surrounded by the Puget Sound.

I remember the fresh garden lettuce and carrots,
Chopped together to make a salad.
The smell of sweet potatoes mixing with roast beef,
Filling the room.

My grandmother cooked applesauce cake,
With efficiency and consistency.

Sometimes I was invited to stir the soup,
And other times I would make the whole meal.
And I always knew I had a place in the kitchen.

As I grew, I discovered that kitchens could also be fun and peaceful.
And I found joy in creating places of welcome and warmth.

Today in my kitchen you'll find the KitchenAid mixer on the granite countertop,
With my favorite wooden spoon from my time in Ghana standing by.

Sausage and cabbages sauteing is something I treasure in our kitchen, with bubbles and squeaks you can hear.
The sizzling mingles with the smell of caraway and dill as our Christmas Eve meal is made.

While some days my kitchen is a place I barely run through on the way out the door,
There is always hope for peace and presence as I long to be part of creating a more just and generous world.

WHAT DO YOU BRING TO YOUR KITCHEN? (DERRICK)

The first kitchen counter I remember is white laminate,
In my grandparents' home.
My grandfather is cooking there,
Hands stirring, and jokes coming from his lips.

Our home was on the land with a walnut tree and all kinds of birds,
In an urban neighborhood,
Surrounded by other homes and near the local playground.

I remember the bread and cheese,
Melting together to make grilled cheese sandwiches.
The smell of chicken mixing with greens,
Filling the room.

My mother cooked macaroni and cheese
With grace and generosity.

Sometimes I was invited to stir batter,
And other times I stood back and watched.
And I always knew something good was coming!

As I grew, I discovered that kitchens could also be calm and reflective.
And I found peace in creating places of hospitality and fellowship.

Today in my kitchen you'll find a scale on the wooden counter, with a bread knife
    nearby.

You'll also find a basil and olive oil blend to make pesto.
The sound of water boiling mingles with the smell of freshly grated cheese as dinner is
    being made.

While some days my kitchen is chaotic,
There is always hope for order coming from the chaos.
As I long to be part of creating a more compassionate and convivial world.

THE KITCHEN AS A KEEPER OF STORIES

As we began writing this book, we gained clarity around what we hoped it would be. Rather than a recitation of facts, ingredients, and figures, we have aimed as much as possible to offer you a collection of understandings about your food story. Every week, we and our friend Sam ask our guests on *The Food and Faith Podcast*, "What is your geography—the people, places, food, music, and culture that have made you who you are?"

We love the responses we get. People often comment on how much richer a question it is than "Tell us about where you're from." And whether we discuss personal stories or larger political constructs, history often comes up when talking about food. This is one of the powerful aspects of the kitchen; it can become a repository for the stories of our pasts. The kitchen holds the stories of our families as well as the stories of our nation. Our kitchens keep the secrets passed through generations and those we thought were lost to time.

Map Your Kitchen

What is the geography of your kitchen?

What geographies did the kitchen of your childhood hold?

Imagine you are back in that kitchen space:

What foods are on the counters?

What smells fill the air?

Who is cooking?

Who is gathered for conversation?

How do you feel, being in the kitchen?

Many of our interviewees shared the geography of the kitchen in the home in which they grew up. The kitchens are as diverse as the people describing them. Among those who demonstrate the ways personal and cultural histories are lived out in the kitchen are two of the voices you'll meet throughout the book. Our friend and fellow food enthusiast Justin Cox is an American Baptist pastor. He and his family currently live in New England, but his roots are in Appalachian North Carolina. In researching Appalachian cooking—what he describes as chasing nostalgia—he taps into the nostalgia of people, like Ronni Lundy, author of *Shuck Beans, Stack Cakes, and Honest Fried Chicken: The Heart and Soul of Southern Country Kitchens* and many other cookbooks. Lundy's cornbread recipe brought Justin back to his childhood. "I'm going to try not to tear up talking about it," he said to us. "When I made that cornbread and pulled it out of that skillet, I knew when I flipped it onto a plate, it was the same color . . . it was the same texture. I put it in my mouth, and it was every afternoon when I was a kid and I would get to my grandmother's house to watch *Teenage Mutant Ninja Turtles* on the big dial television."

Another recurring voice in our book is Kendall Vanderslice, the creator of the Edible Theology Project, a nonprofit educational media project with the goal of bringing people together around the table to talk about food stories both global and personal, theological and practical. Kendall understands the power of storytelling in the kitchen and builds opportunities to share personal and family histories. She describes ways that baking encourages the sharing of stories. When baking bread with children as a way to explore aspects of faith, she says, "we talk about how food tells stories and how the food that we eat connects us to our family, that it connects us to our grandparents. It might connect us to the place that we came from, or the place that our parents came from. So we encourage the kids to think about some of the stories that their family might tell through food. And one of the activities is creating a menu that helps to tell the story of who you are."

AN INVITATION TO HOPE

Life has real demands. Our time is often limited, we have to think about what our kids will and will not eat, or maybe we're tired of cooking for just ourselves. And sometimes we just want to order pizza. That's real! We don't expect that anything we are writing will automatically turn your kitchen into a magical place of Zen. What we do hope—and, as we've said, hope is a big aspect of the just kitchen for us—is that in small, incremental ways, we can support each other in showing reverence to the space that nourishes us and those we love. And in that hope is a lot of grace.

As throughout the book we'll share kitchen insights and stories from diverse people, we hope you find voices that resonate for you. They are people who care deeply about the state of the world, and who often find space to bring that deep care into their reflections on their kitchens. Each story or insight is meant to draw our attention back to the kitchen as we invite you to explore your own histories and hopes for a just kitchen. We're on this exploration together with you. We don't have all the answers, but we have a lot of very good questions, and we hope you'll find something nourishing in the questions as we together seek to nurture a more just and generous world.

WHAT GIVES YOU HOPE?
Justin Cox

The kitchen is where I get centered. If there is a day that I don't bake or don't cook, it feels weird. Cooking is a never-ending conversation about the small things: failing at a recipe, getting mad because it didn't turn out right or the bread didn't rise in the middle. It's constant—knowing that I'm never going to get it right. But I get a little bit closer. I can get close to right. I think that is hopeful.

The small things give me hope too. Like reaching into my refrigerator and finding three or four mason jars, unlabeled, full of sauces and things that I've tried to make. I'm not pulling out Heinz ketchup; I'm pulling out some kind of barbecue sauce that was cooked for an hour on my stove, and I get to give it to somebody. And then every time I pull out the jar I kept for myself, I think of the person I gave some to: "I put it on my hot dogs the other day, and I really enjoyed it," they told me. And it's hopeful that we're going to come back together and share these stories.

And then maybe all the things that we shared on private doorsteps, we can move to the front lawns of our churches. Imagine a big table out in the front of our church where we can sit and talk. I'm really hoping we can discuss in my community putting picnic tables out on our church lawn because there are only a few big community-focused places in our town. They are landmarks. One is a general store, which has a lunch counter and people usually sit outside, but there's not a lot of space. So I'm hopeful about the power of sitting and eating with people. Food can allow us to have picnic tables up around our church, and people can stop in and share a meal together and break bread in some form.

And I'm hopeful I'm just going to stumble on a chef and think, *Oh, my God, I can't believe I didn't know about them. I need to read this book, or I need to reach out.* When I stumbled on Kendall Vanderslice and her work on edible theology, we started using that at our church—some edible theology for kids. And there's hope in what you and others are doing. Knowing you're not alone. You're not in a bubble. And maybe you're still a black sheep, but you've got a flock. I get hope from finding other people who are doing their work. And my hope is that I'm giving them some life too.

Dood's Table Biscuits—A Pinched Method

Justin Cox

My grandmother, Dood (a nickname), was well polished in the kitchen. She sought proficiency, and her biscuits were an example of this. She was known to say, "They aren't fancy, but my family likes them." Many afternoons my sister and I would eat these biscuits right after we got off the school bus. They have become a staple in our home, as I make them for my family and neighbors several times a week.

Recipe

INGREDIENTS

A seasoned cast-iron skillet with a tablespoon or more of bacon drippings to coat the pan

300 grams self-rising flour (I like Guilford Mill or White Lily)

1/2 teaspoon salt

1 stick frozen butter, grated

1 cup buttermilk (*Not a bad idea to keep extra flour and buttermilk handy*)

DIRECTIONS

1. Preheat your oven to 450 degrees.
2. Coat your skillet with bacon drippings.
3. In a decent size bowl, whisk your flour and salt together. Add in your grated butter. Pour in buttermilk.
4. I use a spatula to combine the wet and dry ingredients, making sure to pull in the dough that might want to stick to the inside of the mixing bowl. Once you have a nice clump of dough, dust the top with some extra flour. Flour your hands as the dough will probably want to stick to your fingers.
5. "Pinch" off a piece and lightly mold it into a biscuit-like shape. Place biscuits in the skillet, slightly touching one another until you run out of room. Place in your oven.
6. I typically bake them for 15–17 minutes, rotating the skillet at the halfway point. Brush with salted butter and serve.

LITURGY
Who Is and Was and Is to Come

Holy God,
Holder of our stories,
Come to us now.

God of our ancestors,
Come to us now.

God of this present moment,
Come to us now.

God of the generations that are yet to be,
Come to us now.

Usher us into a new possibility,
Inspire us to take a chance for change,
Kindle in us the hunger for justice,
And nourish us with your love.

Amen.

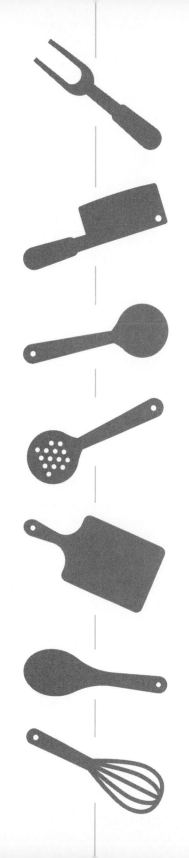

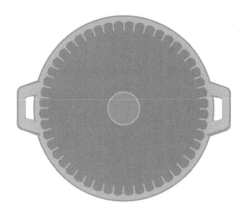

CHAPTER 2

THE KITCHEN AS A PLACE OF INTERACTION

Choosing our food based on where it has been before it hits our kitchen is one of the bigger political decisions we make every day. We get to decide how we spend our money and time, and what impact these choices make. In a sense, before we discuss the kitchen itself, we have to take a detour outside our home, looking at the ways we source our food and how cooking has a ripple effect.

Food is the primary way we relate to the natural world. In fact, eating relationships are the primary way most species interact with each other. Yes, there are symbiotic relationships in which smaller animals hitch a ride on larger animals, and plant species that use others to pollinate or germinate. (Apparently fungi talk to each other underground, which is weird and cool.) But how we relate to each other in the food web is the main way living things connect.

It's not something many of us humans like to think about. We prefer to think of our connection to nature happening through a walk in the woods or a swim in a lake.

We have pets and houseplants that give us the sense that we have tamed nature enough to bring it into our homes, and landscaping to give us a sense of controlling what's outside. Despite all these other interactions, there is no more intimate relationship that we have to the "natural world" than through what we eat—and what eats us (more things than we care to admit).

Rev. Dr. Christopher Carter, an associate professor at the University of San Diego and a Methodist pastor whose work centers on racial justice, firmly grasps how food creates interactions between human communities both now and across time periods: "The foods that preserve and promote community, the foods that are wrapped up in the stories that we share . . . have shifted over time, not only within American history, but [within] human history." He recognizes that we need to be intentional about what we eat because of its impact on the nonhuman world, where that impact may determine what we eat in the future. "In this era of climate change," he says, "I'd be lying if I said I wasn't scared for what my son will be able to eat in the future. Teaching about eating with intention is what's going to hopefully allow my son to survive."

A BRIEF HISTORY OF FOOD

The history of food is the history of humans making decisions about which species of plants and animals were (a) edible, (b) easy to cultivate, and (c) the right balance of nutritious and delicious. Certain species were bred for certain qualities. Corn, for example, is a grass that was continually cultivated to have larger and larger edible seeds. In the industrialized world, we have stretched the limits of this "optimization" with genetically modified organisms (GMOs). The ability to breed and feed a chicken with hormones to create an oversized and salable breast is an extreme example of what humans have been doing since the beginning of agriculture.

But this cultivated interaction between humans and other species isn't one-sided. Being pleasing to animal senses is one of the ways plant species themselves evolve to stay alive. Sweeter fruit and stronger fragrances allow for greater probability of seed-spreading and pollination. And most domesticated animal species have been bred over the centuries to a point where they would have difficulty surviving without human intervention. Mutuality undeniably exists in the natural world, and part of human nature is to create that mutuality with other species. As Michael Pollan writes in *The Botany of Desire: A Plant's-Eye View of the World*, "We . . . are partners in a coevolutionary relationship, as indeed we have been since the birth of agriculture more than ten thousand years ago."

Yes, we are a part of an ecosystem, but part of the problem with our food system is that we don't always see ourselves as part of a whole. In fact, we are a vital part of the food web, our role made all the more crucial because of the potential impacts, both positive and negative, that we have on our environment. Nonhuman species respond to us and adapt as best they can. A vital shift in our food system could take place if we began seeing ourselves as a part of nature. When we do, we begin to see how we bring foods to our kitchen differently, and our kitchens become more just as we, in Chris Carter's words, learn and teach through *intention*.

Soil and Nature: On the Garden
Anna's Story

I don't think everyone needs to be a gardener, but I sure do hope that everyone gets to at least hang out in a garden now and again. Something changes in my very being when I put my hands in the soil and see how nature miraculously brings life and food out of tiny seeds.

I first started growing vegetables in our family garden when I was about five years old. My mother wisely suggested radishes as a first attempt, and though I didn't particularly love the taste then, nor do I now, I remember the great satisfaction I found when those little seeds popped up and turned into food.

I have been gardening ever since. For much of my adult life it's been in containers on apartment decks or in little spots dug out by a townhouse, or in grow bags circling a shared house. Only in the last year, at age forty-three, do I finally have a real yard with the space to put in raised beds and a proper veggie garden. Some folks I know say they don't have a green thumb and ask how I do it. I just say, "Try something." Our neighbors, who we shared a grow-bag garden with in our last home, kept tending a portion of the garden after we moved. To our delight, and theirs too it seems, they caught the bug and put in a garden the next year and are already talking about what they can do at the home they just bought that has a yard.

Growing food has brought me closer to nature, but it has also brought me closer to the people who grow and pick and transport all the food that I don't grow in our garden. Engaging in the growing of food, in whatever way, invites us into a reverence for this miracle—and the accompanying labor—that goes into bringing food to our kitchens.

HOW DOES FOOD CONNECT US TO OUR COMMUNITIES?

Food is also a primary way that we interact with other humans. Humans grow food for each other, cook food for each other, transport food to one another, and employ each other to do all these activities. As we saw earlier, food has also long been a part of the systems that allow for human oppression—but it can just as easily be a part of human liberation. What happens in our kitchens is a means by which we not only contact the natural world but also relate to many people who often go unseen.

Most of us are largely disconnected from the people who grow and raise our food. Generally speaking, this seems to be something we've just grown to accept, yet not too long ago the idea of not knowing the farmer, rancher, or fisher responsible for getting food to our kitchen would have been preposterous. Now the growing of our food, and to a large extent the cooking of our food, has been outsourced to big corporate entities.

The term "factory farm" gets used a lot, particularly by those of us who care about where food comes from. That is neither our expertise nor the point of this book, but it's important to mention. Simply put, during the Nixon administration of the early 1970s, the secretary of agriculture had a clear message to farmers: "Get big or get out!" The motive was to have cheap food readily available for the American public, and for the most part, it worked. Since then, Americans have spent a lower percentage of their income on food than any society in history. Corporations produce food primarily through systems of monoculture, meaning one large piece of land dedicated to one species—whether corn, wheat, pigs, cows, and so on. It may make food affordable, but it harms the land, as ecosystems thrive on diversity. To replace the nutrients lost to the soil by overgrowing a single crop in one space, we use chemical fertilizers. To boost the immune systems of animals crowded into pens, we fill them with antibiotics. To get crops from farms to the stores where they are sold, which may be thousands of miles away, we spray them with preservatives or seal them in plastic, and load them into trucks, boats, and planes burning tons of fossil fuels. This is the system the majority of us have bought into—and sometimes necessarily so as affordability of food determines what we are able to purchase. Yet the results have increased in diet-related diseases such as diabetes, obesity, and hypertension, the continued erosion of our soils, and increasing climate change.

Knowing how factory farming and our evolving food systems are harming humans and the larger environment can lead us to paralysis or despair—and even more so for many of us who feel affordability is our only option on a tight budget. But we lead here with hope and an invitation to think about how each of our individual kitchens can be part of the movement toward a more just world overall. Some of us can take bigger steps, some of us tiny ones, but even the tiny movement toward a more just kitchen is a meaningful step.

WHERE DOES OUR FOOD COME FROM?

Sourcing food is an obvious need before we cook. In our interviews and in our own lives, we are struck by how different personalities engage differently in the shopping, growing, and sourcing of food. Some menu-plan for a week at a time, make a list, and then shop. Others wander the aisles of the grocery store, looking for what's on sale and being inspired from there. Many of us are trying to get more in touch with the rhythms of the seasons and with eating what is currently growing in the climate around us locally. Many enjoy participating in farmers' markets, community-supported agriculture (CSA) produce boxes, and community gardens—some of which offer sliding-scale purchases or double-purchase points, making items more affordable. Wherever, or in whatever combination of places, you source your food from, we invite you into the practice of paying attention not only to the sources but to the stories behind the food because each peach, perch, or slice of pepperjack has a story.

We spoke with author Virginia (Ginny) Messina, who offered many suggestions (as she does in her coauthored book, *Protest Kitchen*) about how cooking reflects care for the world around her. "In a protest kitchen, you might choose, if you have the ability, to cook more from scratch or eat from your own garden. . . . I'm looking at factory farms and thinking about ways you can remove your participation in them, or at least decrease your participation in them." While holding to these principles, Ginny acknowledges how difficult it can be to create a harm-free kitchen. "Even as a vegan who is very conscious about my food choices, I am just appalled by how much plastic goes through my kitchen!"

Whether or not to eat meat often becomes one of the central questions in thinking about the ways our cooking affects our communities. Like many things in our world, people of similar convictions can reach different conclusions about what a solution might look like. But it's an important question to wrestle through.

TO EAT MEAT OR NOT TO EAT MEAT—THAT IS A QUESTION

Neither of us has chosen to be vegan, but we have learned a lot from Ginny Messina and her writing partner, Carol J. Adams, who are both vegans. As we spoke with them, they kind-heartedly and generously communicated the "why" of their veganism in compelling ways. At the heart of it, their veganism stems from a desire to interact positively with their communities, the larger food system, and the rest of creation.

In *Protest Kitchen: Fight Injustice, Save the Planet, and Fuel Your Resistance One Meal at a Time*, they speak to their stance on the importance of what happens in the kitchen. Ginny explained the thinking that went into the book: "We started talking about what veganism meant to us and what our food choices meant to us. . . . Food choices are really a part of fighting back against regressive politics. We make food choices that impact the environment, we make food choices that impact farmworkers, and we make food choices that impact so many things that people aren't thinking about."

Rev. Dr. Christopher Carter, also a vegan, said veganism is part of an ethic he defines as *soulful eating*. "I call it 'soulful eating' because it takes broad things into consideration beyond what's merely on the plate. I became deeply convicted about the ways in which I was talking about liberation and how I could see the connection between the oppression of nonhuman nature and the oppression of Black folks. It was super obvious in ways which unsettled me." In response to the oppression he observed, Chris adopted the philosophy of Black Veganism, a movement that has been growing in popularity in the last decade. "My veganism is for the people. It really is for me to be in solidarity with marginalized people, particularly people of color."

For our vegan friends and many others, there is great concern for the ways that what happens in the kitchen impacts their neighbors—local and global, human and nonhuman. For them, the kitchen is a place of local and global interaction and interconnectedness.

Chris's work points us to another casualty of our food system: farmworkers. Farmworkers often endure deplorable conditions, particularly in concentrated animal feeding operations (CAFOs), where animals are raised in large numbers for meat, or in the slaughterhouses where they are processed. These facilities are disproportionately staffed by people of color working for low wages. "If we're going to take seriously the impact that industrial agriculture, particularly animal agriculture, has on Black bodies, we ought to opt out of it," says Chris. He believes that because factory farms are often located in places that aren't easily seen by the general public, we lose sight of what is happening inside the facilities. "It's easy to lose sight of their humanity. So how can we take their humanity seriously? I'm suggesting we need to opt out of these systems."

Jake Marquez and Maren Morgan, a young couple from Salt Lake City, Utah, are producers of the podcast *Death in the Garden*. Both Maren and Jake had experiences that led them briefly to become vegan. While both abandoned veganism for health reasons, they acknowledge that the ethic that led to their giving up animal products came from good intentions. "The intentions of many vegans," Jake explained, "are the most beautiful intentions ever. My only gripe comes when those things get formed into a rigid ideology." As you might intuit from the name of their podcast and film, Maren and Jake are largely concerned with the disconnect between the food in our kitchens and the death required to bring that food there. Maren argues that taking the life of an animal can be a deeply spiritual experience. "When you take the life of an animal and you feel the exchange, that is a really beautiful experience. There is no cruelty in it. But there is cruelty in having one person kill one thousand cows a day." She believes that we all need to "have access to taking responsibility for the death of animals."

Rev. Karen Mann is a pastor in the United Church of Christ and also a farmer near Charlottesville, Virginia. Rev. Mann shares much of this sentiment and speaks passionately about the animals in her care and about the realities of eating the animals she raises. "I want people to know that every time I take a pig to the butcher, I look that animal in the eye, and I honor that animal, and I pray that their end will come swiftly and as painlessly as possible. And it's important to me that I look them in the eye every time." For Rev. Mann, to forget that her meat is produced at the cost of a life would be unethical.

While neither of us is vegan, there are values we appreciate and share with our vegan friends. First, most Americans—from both a justice and a health perspective—could stand to eat less meat. We are the only nation that expects to eat all three meals a day with meat as the central focus. Second, animals raised for meat should be cared for as lovingly as possible. As Rev. Mann says, her animals have "one bad day." Finally, there needs to be an acknowledgment that something has to die for us to eat. Even growing the monocultures ultimately aimed at becoming a meat substitute displaces a large amount of wildlife. And let's face it: though we value plants' lives differently, they also die in order for us to live. Interactions between species often involve the death of one. It's better, in our view, to acknowledge and honor this exchange of life than to ignore it. And it's better to make sure that the life taken in order for us to eat is taken with honor and reverence for what is sacrificed.

Even those who choose veganism acknowledge the further ethical issues. Because of the harmful effects of chemicals used in agriculture, choosing to forgo meat doesn't necessarily avoid ethical pitfalls. A "100% certified organic" label is a start toward knowing that good farming practices were used. But that sticker doesn't mean your zucchini didn't travel thousands of miles on a truck spitting out carbon into the environment to get to you.

EATING LOCALLY

It may seem quaint or old-fashioned, but one of the easiest ways to feel good about the produce entering the house is to know a farmer. Farmers' markets, community-supported agriculture, and community gardens make this a bit easier. They give you opportunities to ask about pesticide and herbicide use, learn how far away your food was grown, find out what is in season—and, in the case of community gardens, enjoy the additional opportunity of growing your own.

Shopping seasonally is one of the ways we push back against the corporate system of agriculture. Both of us live in the American Northeast; there really is no way we should have access to bananas in January, even as a factory agricultural system says that folks in cold climates can have tropical fruits any time they want so long as they are willing to ignore the thousands of miles the produce had to travel from Mexico, Hawaii, or Chile.

Of course, the shortest distance food can travel is from your backyard or your apartment planters to your kitchen. Both of us are gardeners and know both the joys and frustrations of growing our own food. Most of us have extreme limitations on what we can grow and when, but those limitations shouldn't discourage us from growing something. Gardening is a lovely act of rebellion against a corporate food system, and when we add things like seed-saving, seed-swapping, and produce exchanges, we can have a small but real impact on the food system in our local community.

And before you argue that you don't have a green thumb or that you live in an apartment with no space, allow us to enlighten you: there's no such thing as not being able to garden! The ability to grow food isn't some magical gift that some of us have. Yes, it takes some skill. Yes, it takes patience. And yes, sometimes you'll need to bike to your local community garden to do the planting, and will want to understand basic soil fertility and health. But mostly it requires the ability to read the back of a seed packet, an ability you've already demonstrated by reading this far in this book!

Experiment. Get to know your growing zone and what does well there. Talk to other gardeners. Google stuff. Whatever you do, don't let some mystical notion of who can and can't grow things stand in your way.

And know, like us, that we all fall short of our ideals when it comes to sourcing our foods and bringing them to our kitchens as places of interaction. But sourcing our meat locally as much as possible, going to farmers' markets whenever we can, and growing what we have time to grow make a small, but valuable, dent in our food consumption.

With two working adults, plus children, in each of our families, convenience and price are always considerations. That's not an excuse, just a reality. If you're feeling the tension between the ideals and the reality, we're with you.

Pollan's Food Rules

After Michael Pollan wrote *In Defense of Food: An Eater's Manual*, he followed it up with a short book titled *Food Rules: An Eater's Manual*, in which he lists some guidelines we can use when shopping for our food. Amid the longer list of guidelines are these points we find particularly helpful:

1. Eat only foods that will eventually rot.

2. Get out of the supermarket: buy at CSAs and farmers' markets.

3. Eat foods made *from* a plant, not *in* a plant.

4. (If you choose to eat meat) Eat animals that have eaten well themselves.

5. Avoid food products that are overprocessed, containing more than five ingredients.

It's hard to break away from the industrial food system. While we don't believe we can save the world solely through better consumerism, to the extent we must participate in the larger corporate food system we can make good decisions within it. In his *In Defense of Food: An Eater's Manual*, Pollan suggests we shop the perimeters of the grocery store to avoid ultra-processed foods. Paying attention to and making food choices based on levels of organic certification on produce, as well as animal welfare certifications on meat, shows producers that there is market demand for more ethically produced foods. When we each do little things to break away from the corporate system, as well as speaking up for those abused by it, it adds up to significant impact.

Your Garden—the Closest Source
Derrick's Story

I desperately wish that my kitchen was filled with produce I had grown. Cooking with food you've grown yourself comes with a sense of accomplishment that grocery shopping just can't provide. It's remarkable to see something through the process from seed to plate. Alas, growing your own food is hard when it's not your full-time job. Hell, it's hard when it is your full-time job. That said, I think we should all try to grow what we can.

My journey into caring deeply about food started with a garden. For years I had a little container garden where I sometimes got enough basil for pesto, and occasionally had a tomato or two to add to a salad or a sandwich. When I had the opportunity for a larger garden plot, I had romantic ideas about growing a significant percentage of the food my family eats. In hindsight, that was hilarious! You have to have multiple plants of any food you want to eat to get enough for a meal. That's assuming you don't lose your plants to too much rain, not enough rain, bugs, chipmunks, bunnies, deer, birds, bacteria, fungi, or your own neglect.

I'm now at the point where I supply most of my family's herbs, though not enough to keep up with our house's voracious demand for pesto. I usually get a good haul of tomatoes and potatoes, enough to make salsa and sauce from the former and a couple rounds of hash browns from the latter. We get a couple of salads' worth of lettuce, greens that usually only I will eat (unless I sneak them into the aforementioned pesto), the occasional scrawny carrot, and, on average, three edible asparagus spears annually. I've somehow gotten proficient at growing butternut squash, much to the dismay of my family.

I happen to believe that the food I grow tastes better than the food I get from the produce section of the grocery store, though I have no studies to back this up. But I do know that food we take care to grow ourselves travels the least number of miles and reduces the percentage of greenhouse gas produced in transporting food. The food we produce ourselves is largely healthier, assuming we aren't dousing plants in pesticides.

SEEKING SOLIDARITY WITH THOSE WHO FEED US

One of the reasons we love to talk about food is because it can be unifying. We all have to eat! We've seen how structures of power can divide us into a serving class and a class of people being served, but one of the goals of recognizing how food connects us with the land and with a larger food system is to acknowledge our interdependence. We've seen through the COVID-19 pandemic just how vital the seemingly invisible workforce that grows and delivers our food really is. We have a vivid example of how undervalued they often are. As the pandemic raged in 2020, then-President Trump issued an executive order to keep meatpacking plants operating despite the fact that those frontline workers were more exposed to the virus than most of the population. People's lives were put at risk so we could eat!

Understanding our food system isn't just about our own health and that of our families; it is about the health of those who work in hard conditions, growing, picking, feeding, packing, shipping, and delivering the items we eat. While opting out of the larger food system when we can is important, we should not do so at the expense of forgetting those who keep that system moving. A just kitchen calls for us to advocate for unions that protect the most vulnerable in the food system: farmworkers. We need to enact immigration policies that won't allow for the exploitation of pickers and growers. We need labor laws that protect people in factories. We need a farm bill that keeps smaller farms from being swallowed by large corporations.

By and large, the parts of our government that control the food system are the most bipartisan working bodies in the country. No one in power wants to disrupt the power structures of the food system. But that means that the rights of workers and growers are largely ignored as the recurring US Farm Bill, a bill that mostly works to maintain the status quo of relatively cheap food, is renewed approximately every five years. What happens in our kitchens is a type of vote for the kind of food system we want, but we must remember that our actual votes are important as well. Something as large and important as our food system deserves far more conversation and, yes, debate than it usually receives.

Gary Nabhan, an author, activist, and ethnobotanist, recently wrote a book titled *Jesus for Farmers and Fishers: Justice for All Those Marginalized by Our Food System*. Gary uses beautiful retranslations of Jesus's parables to remind us of the agrarian setting of early Palestine and that many of Jesus's followers were a part of the hierarchical food system of his time. Nabhan uses a stunning reimagination of the beatitudes to help bring those who are often forgotten by our system back into clear focus:

- Blessed are those who hunger and thirst especially at the margins of the greatest surplus of food in the history of the world.
- Blessed are those who flip burgers in fast food drive-ins, who fill burritos in taco trucks, and who go from house to house with coolers of homemade goods hidden in their trunks.
- Blessed are those who patch together their shelters from pallets and tarps.
- Blessed are those who glean their meals from the produce dumped on the edge of fields.
- Blessed are those who are famished and fatigued when nightfall comes.
- Blessed are those who pray for Jesus to arrive with fresh loaves and fishes.
- Blessed are those who live with the fear that Immigration and Naturalization Service will show up with handcuffs and paddy wagons to deport them.

CONNECTED IN LOVE

Becoming attuned to and aware of where our food comes from and who and what has been part of its journey to our kitchens can be part of our spiritual practice in the kitchen. A spiritual practice some folks use regularly in a blessing of the food, or as a conversation piece at the beginning of the meal, is to share where each food item has come from. In our households, we can often be found following up our blessing song with a little geography tracing of what is on our plate: "Everything in the salad is from our garden, except for the tomatoes, which came from the farmers' market. The sausage is from Aldi's, and the bread is from the bakery downtown." This simple practice is one that encourages both attentiveness and gratitude. One can take it a step further and research the companies of the food purchased at the store, learn about food workers' rights, and think about the environmental impact even one meal has.

For those of us who are religious and spiritual, giving thanks before digging in is often part of this blessing process. It is an opportunity to consider the Divine present and moving in all things—even our food. In Christian tradition, the invitation to engage with an incarnational God is closely intertwined with the possibility of our kitchens being places of healing, interconnection, and hope.

Remembering that God is in all things, from the body of the exploited farmworker to the pig about to be slaughtered, brings to mind that all of creation is connected and interacts. In one of the gospel texts about Jesus, there's a beautiful line: "And the Word became flesh and dwelt among us"—and the Greek word for "flesh" that the Word (*Logos*) became is *sarx*, related to words like "earth," "earthly," "fellow humans," and "kindred." To become "flesh" is to become material reality—matter itself.

The Divine, the Logos, the divine utterance, makes itself visible here and now in the natural world. It dwells among us. The paraphrase of the text from *The Message* reads, "The Word became flesh and blood, and moved into the neighborhood." Even while we are in our kitchens, we meet the Divine moving in all things that connect us to the rest of creation and humanity. God is always trying to make love visible, tangible, and present. Love is always urging and pressing to be received, never forcing itself on us but stirring our hearts, moving in our longings, inviting us to draw toward and be vessels of the Light, connecting us to others. And the continued miracles pulse through our faith stories and traditions throughout time, impressing upon us that divine Love is right here, right now, breaking into the world, breaking into our kitchens with justice.

In the gardens around us, as plants stretch their roots down and leaves and flowers reach for the sun, we can see this force at work. In our kitchens, when we are paying attention to where the food we are preparing came from and how the land and animals and people contributed to it, we see this force alive in people working for good in the world, including those working to promote food sovereignty and environmental healing. In the love we see among community and neighbors and family and friends, we witness that connecting force.

We see and feel this in-breaking of the love and light when we look into each other's faces across the table, when we welcome someone we don't know into our lives, and when we go outside our comfort zone to engage another human being.

And this in-breaking goes so much further than that—it goes out to the broken bodies, the battered hearts, the abused land. Love is constantly pushing and urging and renewing and healing. And this love calls us back into our kitchens, to pay attention to how we are connected, to think about how the Divine is present in the food we are about to prepare, and how God is using our engagement with this food as an opportunity to be part of that love and justice shared in the world.

WHAT GIVES YOU HOPE?
Christopher Carter

To me, the virtue of hope sits between the vices of despair and cynicism that nothing is going to be good, so, whatever. And to me, hope is also a presumption—which has a lot to do with the way I was raised in the Black church—that everything's going to work out, because it's all part of God's plan. That was the kind of language we heard growing up.

I didn't resonate with that because I experienced too much craziness growing up. I felt like, no, this doesn't seem consistent with the God I know in the Bible. God's plan is not for me to have all this suffering.

So, what gives me hope is my recognition that hope comes from the transformation I think is possible in the human condition. I look at my grandfather, and I see the fact that a man who's almost ninety years old wakes up every day with a particular kind of gratefulness that is just astonishing. Even though many of his experiences were absolutely terrible, he says, "Load me up this morning!"

That's the kind of language he has; he's glad he's able to be here. He has a particular positive outlook, but he's also a realist—he understands what's happening. But he also understands that so many of his colleagues and friends and family didn't make it. And so he's grateful—legitimately grateful—that he feels like God has blessed him to be.

That gratefulness gives me hope. I can continue to do the work I feel God has called me to do. And I believe that I can do it in a way that doesn't wear me down or make me feel burned out and that gives me life and is life-affirming.

My son is another reason for hope. He's what gives me the will to do the work. I want my son to inherit a space and a place that allows him to flourish as a multiracial child, as a big child. My son is going to be a big, Black man. He comes from a family of tall folks. And what is the planet going to be like for him?

So I think my hope is centered on those kinds of spaces and on my commitment to live the call that God's placed upon me and to embody that call. It's a theological answer. I believe in my prayer life and in my worship life and in the relationship I've cultivated with the Divine. And, as the church elders will say, like Jeremiah, there is a fire in my bones. I can't *not* do this work. There have been times when I would have preferred not to do this work, but I can't not do it, so I'm living it out.

Red Beans and Rice

From *The Spirit of Soul Food: Race, Faith, and Food Justice*, by Christopher Carter

──────── **Recipe** ────────

INGREDIENTS

1 tablespoon grapeseed oil (or any high-heat oil)

1 large onion, diced medium

6 6-inch celery stalks, diced small

6 garlic cloves, minced

4 vegan sausages (recommended: Field Roast Vegetarian Grain Meat sausages, either smoked apple sage, Italian, or Mexican chipotle flavor)

1 teaspoon chili powder

1 teaspoon Cajun seasoning

1 teaspoon dried thyme

4 cups broth made from Better Than Bouillon seasoned vegetable base

2 15-ounce cans kidney beans, rinsed and drained

1 red bell pepper, cored, seeded, and chopped

2 cups cooked basmati rice

1/2 cup green onion

DIRECTIONS

1. Heat a 4- or 5-quart stew pot over high heat, add oil, and wait until it shimmers.
2. Add onion and celery and cook, stirring with a wooden spoon, until translucent, about 10 minutes. Add the garlic and cook about 2 minutes more. Add the sausage, chili powder, Cajun seasoning, thyme, broth, beans, and bell pepper.
3. Bring to a simmer and cook for 10–15 minutes, stirring frequently.
4. Season with salt, pepper, and your favorite hot sauce.
5. Serve over a bed of rice, and garnish with green onion.

LITURGY
Tracing Blessing

Abundant God,
We thank you for this meal.
We thank you:

For the earth that nourished it,
Especially [name some of the places and soils where the food was
grown and raised].

For the people who planted and watered and cared for it,
Especially [name the people, or groups of people, who farmed
your food].

For those who picked it and transported it to our kitchen,
Especially [name the groups and individuals who harvested and
transported your food].

For those who prepared and cooked,
Especially [name those in your kitchen and those before your
kitchen who prepared and cooked your food].

Holy God, we thank you for the gift of eating and being fed,
And we pray for those who cannot say the same this day,
Especially [name those who are experiencing food insecurity and
food apartheid].

As we eat, may this food nourish us to be part of nurturing the
Beloved Community,
Where all are cared for and all are fed.

Amen.

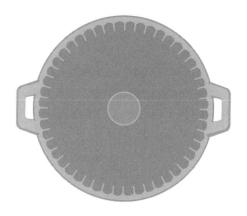

CHAPTER 3

THE KITCHEN AS A PLACE OF PREPARATION

One of the downsides of social media is that it causes us to compare our lives with the versions of other people's lives that they document. It often feels like comparing your bloopers with another person's highlight reel. When it comes to food-related content on social media, there are few things more humbling than watching videos of people setting out their plastic containers, each labeled with a day of the week, and then watching them neatly measure out each day's portion of food with the seeming satisfaction that they have solved one of life's great problems. At least for the week, anyway. The discipline to make such a thing happen is admirable, though one has to wonder how far into the week those preppers get before they abandon ship and hit the drive-thru.

But it's true that before any cooking takes place, preparation is essential. Few of us can walk into a kitchen and improvise like we're playing a jazz solo, but most of us can at least give a moment's consideration to these few essential questions:

- Who am I cooking for?
- How many people am I feeding?
- What foods do they want?
- What foods do they need—or what food restrictions do they have?
- What do I have in my house, kitchen, or pantry already?
- Do I need to go to the store?
- And, of course, how long is this going to take?

Answering all of these questions requires at least a small amount of preparation, but preparation here is not necessarily about being regimented. The discipline to have a weekly menu figured out at the beginning of the week is a must for some, and often reduces a lot of unnecessary stress in the house. But when we talk here about preparation, it's not about regimen or discipline as much as a sense of *intentionality*. Intentionality is about tending to the needs of the people we're going to serve, while balancing our own. It's about creating limits and boundaries for ourselves. Sometimes that limit is a financial budget; sometimes time or dietary restrictions are the limiting factor.

For some, these limits are frustrating; for others, they inspire creativity. We have a friend who talks about how, when she and her family sit down at the table, she enjoys recounting all the "almost gone bad" veggies she used from the refrigerator. The mushrooms that were about to go bad inspire her to search for recipes and form a meal around them. For others, learning to cook without particular allergens becomes a creative challenge, leading to the opening of a new palate of culinary options. Whatever the limitation, good preparation helps us live within the boundaries we set for ourselves, while caring for those at our tables.

PREPARING TO COOK

Writer and speaker Kelley Nikondeha splits her time between Burundi, a small country in East Africa, and the United States. When she travels to Burundi—when she travels anywhere—she puts together her spice order while in transit. "I need the fresh za'atar from Palestine. I need sumac. I need all the Mexican peppers—pequin and aleppo pepper. I need Korean peppers. I need all of the spice mixes and dried peppers."

If you hadn't guessed, Kelley uses tons of spices in her cooking. "I cook mainly Mexican, Italian, and Palestinian foods. Those are the cuisines I lean into. So lots of spices and vinegars and pomegranate molasses and date syrup to embellish and enhance." As an advocate for Palestinian rights, a part of her investment in those foods is an act of solidarity, sometimes sourcing spices from Palestinian vendors when she's there, to support the local economy.

She also loves condiments. The minute she returns from Burundi, she begins preserving lemons, making a batch of shatta—a Palestinian fresh chili condiment. She also likes having pickled onions and pickled carrots ready to go: "I want all the fresh condiments." Her fridge is full of these concoctions, including the labneh she makes fresh every week—a strained yogurt dip used in the Middle East. "I hang it every Sunday night, and then I have fresh labneh throughout the week. I have a lot of fun in the kitchen," she added, smiling.

With such delicious garnishes, condiments, and spices on hand, one can picture how easily Kelley can likely turn simple basics into a feast at a moment's notice.

What do you like to have on hand for the week? One of the best places to start when thinking about preparation is considering what the "must haves" are in your house. Every kitchen's staples look different, but knowing there are a few things that can reliably be found in the fridge or pantry takes at least some of the stress out of getting ready for a meal. What are your go-to spices, condiments, and sauces? What veggies can everyone agree upon? What's the end-of-the-week entrée that will tide you over until the next grocery-shopping trip? Answering these questions can mean the difference between cooking as a joy or a headache.

Perhaps the most important thing we do before we begin to cook—along with making sure we have ingredients we like—is to think about who we're cooking for, even if the answer is ourselves. Cooking for someone assumes a level of knowledge about them. We know their likes. We know their dislikes. We know something about their health status and dietary needs. When Derrick—not a huge fan of brussels sprouts—visited a friend for dinner who knew his love for vegetables and made brussels sprouts the centerpoint, it wasn't a hit. Yet Derrick felt the love of the thoughtful meal, the attention to details and preparation.

Though the nightly preparation for family meals can be a bit monotonous, there is also a joy in knowing what everyone likes and dislikes. There is satisfaction in making one of our partner's favorite dishes, cutting out that one ingredient our picky eater doesn't enjoy, or adding way more cheese to a dish than the recipe calls for because that's the way the family likes it! There is an intimacy that cannot be overlooked in preparing food for our loved ones.

Paying attention to the needs of those who will be eating the food prepared in our kitchen is a continual invitation to intentionality and care. Knowing and cooking within people's dietary needs and preferences is its own act of love and care. It is a way we can see and honor one another's bodies and choices, and celebrate the fact that each of us comes to the table with our own unique hungers.

And when we, or someone in our household, has a reason to change the way eating is done—because of a health need, an allergy, or a choice based on personal ethics—it is an opportunity for reflection and examination. A just kitchen welcomes reflection and examination as we ask ourselves why we cook what we cook, for whom, and what values we uphold in the process. A change in the needs of one person can be a good opportunity to ask questions together.

A story from Anna illustrates that preparation, even for oneself, is an act of love:

One of the first things I ask when inviting someone over for dinner (or even considering our own foods) is whether there is a dietary restriction to be aware of. This isn't simply about avoiding having our guests leave in an ambulance. It's about letting people know they are seen and loved, in their fullness, and that accommodating their needs is not a burden but an opportunity to care for each other by caring for our bodies.

Accepting Boundaries and New Possibilities in the Kitchen
Anna's Story

While the discovery of an allergy or the need to make a dietary change can be daunting, it also can be an invitation to curiosity and creativity. I have had a gluten allergy since my late twenties following a serious illness. Having suffered through being sick for a long stretch of time, it seemed a small thing to give up gluten; I was just grateful to be alive and finding my strength and health again.

But over time, as I got healthier and realized that this allergy was going to be there to stay, I had to come to terms with it in a different way. I found myself longing for the ease and the greasy treat of Friday night pizza delivery. My earlier years of joy in making homemade bread for myself and friends had been abruptly cut off. The sandwich at my favorite deli was no longer an option. And don't get me started on the pasta dishes.

For a while I focused on all the things I couldn't eat. I don't know exactly what changed, but at some point, I found myself shifting my mindset. Rather than focusing on all that was no longer an option, I started to think about what I **could** *eat, and this became a new cooking challenge. Did you know there are delicious cakes that are* **supposed** *to be made with only almond flour? I found that I actually don't need to have a starch made of wheat at every meal. And it turns out that quinoa pasta is delicious.*

PREPARATION AS SELF-CARE

If we are cooking for more mouths than our own, the needs of others will, of course, be a driving concern in our place of preparation. Yet, care for ourselves is a part of preparing for all the others who sit at our table. One of the things we notice when we haven't taken time to do proper preparation is that cooking becomes far more stressful. The feeling of being frantic and anxious about whether you have what you need to pull off your meal just isn't good for you, and likely will affect your own enjoyment of the meal when all is said and done. In a very real way, preparation is caring for our future selves.

A 2015 article from the website *Kitchn* gives five practical suggestions for preparing our kitchen before we even lift a knife or turn on the oven to begin cooking:

1. Read the recipe in its entirety.
2. Clear as much work space as you can.
3. Empty the sink and dishwasher.
4. Find your towels and pot holders.
5. Set out and prep your ingredients.

All these suggestions are about saving sanity and creating ease. There is nothing more frustrating than pushing aside a mess to find a space to work, or discovering in the middle of the food-prep process that the one pot you need is still dirty. Everyone can relate to the sinking feeling of using all of an ingredient in step two, only to find out you were supposed to use "the rest" of that ingredient in step nine. Do we even have to mention how badly things can go when you can't find a pot holder when you need one? Preparation is about being kind both to those you are serving and to yourself.

Preparing to Fail
Derrick's Story

By all accounts, the late, legendary NFL coach Vince Lombardi primarily spoke in motivational poster quotes. One of my all-time favorites of his is: "Those who fail to prepare, prepare to fail." I am married to a planner. Nothing makes my wife feel better than knowing what to expect and when to expect it. This is especially true in the kitchen. We have a dry-erase board on our kitchen door on which are written the prospective meals for the week. If a meal has made it to the dry-erase board, you can all but guarantee we have all the ingredients for said meal, and it's likely that on the morning of the day she plans on making it, the ingredients have been moved out of storage to a more accessible spot in the kitchen.

I am . . . a bit different. I can't tell you how many times I have run to the store in the middle of cooking because I am missing one ingredient. My inability (unwillingness?) to plan meals often leads to the kitchen being left in utter chaos once I have finished cooking. I have been accused of using every single pot and pan when I cook.

While we both can generally take my chaotic kitchen style with good humor, I have become more aware that my lack of planning affects the rest of the family. My impromptu running to the store may delay dinner a half hour. My using every pot and pan puts an additional burden on whoever's turn it is to wash the dishes (and it's usually not the cook). My failing to time out how long it takes for certain things to cook in comparison to other things means sometimes an entrée is cold while a side dish is piping hot. These sound like small things, but planning is part of cooking in a community—a subject we'll explore more in a later chapter—and even just the circle of my own family is a community. Planning is a way to be considerate to the people who share your space and to those who depend on you for meals.

One of the pre-cooking steps mentioned in the Kitchn article referenced above is to clear the sink and dishwasher. Well, one particular evening, I happened to be making pasta. Getting ready to drain the noodles, I realized the sink was filled with dirty dishes. I thought I could wedge a colander into the sink, drain the noodles, and move on with dinner. The scar from the second-degree burn on my left foot reminds me of the valuable lesson of not pouring boiling water into a colander half in, half out of the sink.

Not all my kitchen adjustments have come from painful lessons. A significant change in our house and my cooking came when three of my four children became vegetarians. That means that when the six of us in our blended family are gathered, half are eating meat and the other half are not. We'll continue to talk about the ethics of eating meat throughout this book, but this is simply a place where our family disagrees. I fully respect that my children have made a decision based on what they believe is right, and that they have stuck with this decision with incredible conviction. So, when we are all together, I plan. I either plan a vegetarian option in addition to whatever I'm making, or I make a meatless version of the recipe. There are even occasions when we all eat vegetarian for a night, but that's rare. Yet my kids' dietary choices have made me more conscientious and considerate about meal planning. It's a small way of saying to them that I love them and respect the people they are.

PREPARING WITH A BLESSING

We often think of a blessing as something that happens at the table once the food is prepared and ready to be served. Outside of the food world, though, that isn't usually what it means to "bless" something. A blessing often occurs at the *beginning* of a process: a marriage blessing at a wedding, a travel blessing before a trip, the various blessings used to commission people to forms of communal leadership. These blessings ask for guidance and direction for what lies ahead.

What if part of our preparation to cook was a short blessing, transitioning us from whatever else is going on in our day into the work waiting for us in meal preparation? You might consider saying a blessing prayer before cooking begins. You could include in it an acknowledgment for where the food came from, gratitude for those who made it possible for that food to reach your kitchen, and loving kindness toward all who will gather around your table. Here's one example, but the possibilities are numerous:

> I give thanks for the earth that grew these carrots and the farmers who cultivated them. I give thanks for the animals and those who raised them, and for the folks who transported this beef to the grocery store and to our table. I give thanks for having my daughter at the table tonight. I ask for energy and ease as I prepare this meal.

On days when—let's face it—cooking is not our first choice for how to spend our time, a couple of deep breaths and a time of noticing and blessing can sometimes help shift our attention.

THE KITCHEN AS SANCTUARY AND STUDIO

Our friend Bruce Reyes-Chow, who pastors in Northern California, talks about how the kitchen can be a place of sanctuary for him, a place where he can unwind. He describes the kitchen as an art studio, a tiny world you can control. When asked how the act of preparing food feeds his soul, he shared the following: "I don't know if it's that deep. Yet, there's something about having a kitchen that's yours, that is a place you can control, when you're weighed down by the weight of the world and everything seems so uncontrollable." In the kitchen, he finds a space set apart, a space where he can actually solve the problems in front of him and make an impact on the work that needs to be done. In the kitchen, he's not worried about what other people think—he just gets to create something. "I'll pop on my headphones and listen to something, and I just can be focused in that world for a little bit and not worry about other stuff. There's something about it that grounds me in that space, and I have ultimate control about how things get done."

One line from the familiar Psalm 23 is particularly striking and brings God into the kitchen and to the table: "You prepare a table before me in the presence of my enemies." Bruce's story of that space of comfort and freedom rings true and reminds us that even within a world of struggle, injustice, pain, and, yes, enemies, there are tables prepared where we can find the holy. There are kitchens set apart where we can encounter that which is beyond the chaos of the world.

Bruce prepares his kitchen by making it a place where he can escape the weight of the world, a set-apart sanctuary where he can find peace. For him, cooking is about placing his attention on the details and creating something that is within his purview.

And part of that kitchen-sanctuary for Bruce is the artistic-studio outlet of it as well. He describes how he brings his attention to the act of dicing onions, what they look like; watching the garlic change as it cooks and knowing when it's done; waiting for things to roast in the oven. Each dish brings up particular memories and sensory experiences for him. Like when he makes dim sum: "I'm thinking about my grandmother the whole time. In every cutting, I remember what her stuffing looked like. And so I try to cut the sausage the way that looks like Grandma's." And when he makes a dubow? He thinks of his grandfather: "Granted, we now are using an instant pot," he laughed, "so it's not quite the same. But as I'm preparing the things, I'm taking on my grandfather."

This time apart, this attention to the details, all of this invites a mindset shift when we are preparing in our kitchens. "There is a grounding of now. And there is a grounding of where this all came from that infiltrates all of it," says Bruce.

We often associate *sanctuaries* with religious settings, but for many of us the COVID-19 pandemic and the constant troubling news from all corners of the globe shifted our understanding of the kitchen—we felt the pressing need for our kitchen to feel even more like a sanctuary. And they aren't so different. Both a kitchen and a religious community are places where people, ideally, go to connect with each other, to feel nourished, to serve each other, and to find sustenance for the journey. Bruce reminds us that we have an opportunity, maybe even multiple times a day, to enter our kitchen as a sanctuary—a place for creativity and groundedness in the preparation.

WHEN YOU DON'T HAVE TIME TO PREPARE

Making your kitchen into a special space, where you bless your food and utensils in preparation, all sounds nice, but sometimes that's just not possible. As much as we want this to be about our ideals finding a home in our just kitchen, we also want to create room for grace for when those ideals can't be met. Every night won't be a gourmet meal. Taking it further, sometimes between juggling work, kids, and other responsibilities, you don't have the time or energy to cook. At all.

Many things in our culture have made the kitchen oppressive in the sense of a constant demand for production. It's extractive. We expect to get every dollar's worth of value out of the kitchen, which is often the most expensive room in our home. But from the field of agriculture we've learned what happens when we constantly take from the land without replenishing: we deplete the land of its resources and its ability to nourish us.

In many forms of regenerative agriculture, the solution is to allow the land to go fallow for a season when nothing is used and everything is allowed to lie as it is. Sometimes what is required of us is to let our kitchens be fallow. We need not push ourselves to be constantly producing. That's true in our vocations, but it is true in our homes as well.

Our kitchens need sabbaths as much as our bodies, minds, and spirits do. Those may be the nights when you go out to a restaurant or make sandwiches for supper. Maybe it's a time when you let friends or family cook for you, knowing you'll return the favor when your kitchen feels more inviting. Whatever the solution, it's important that we leave our kitchens for a time. A just kitchen isn't one that demands constant productivity, especially at the expense of our health and sanity. It may simply be the place to make a nourishing cup of tea and allow the pressures on us to be let go.

WHAT GIVES YOU HOPE?
Kelley Nikondeha

This is actually a really difficult question, one I really spent time thinking about. What *does* give me hope? Especially when we think about the kitchen and seasons like Advent and the holidays, there's this sense of a magical, almost glittery filter on life.

Yet the Advent stories that lead to the Christmas story give us hard-won hope, a hope that comes out of the traumatic spaces of life. That informs my sense of what hope is. And it's something I bring into the kitchen. There I connect the spices that come from lands of lament and see hope: Where is the world hurting? Where am I hurting or connecting with that hurt in the world? I trust that there are the seeds of hope in those spaces. And I pray into them in my kitchen, which reflects so many aspects of the world living in the hard-won hope.

This morning I was thinking about the rampant gun violence in our communities. How can we not lament that? Where are the seeds of hope in that? I'm looking to the hard part to say, "How do we redeem this wretchedly violent culture that we live in?"

I think about the malnourishment numbers in Burundi, where the organization my husband and I founded has been part of offering fortified porridge for close to seven years now. We have seen kids who would have died otherwise now running around and healthy, or making their way toward health.

Hope is not a quick hit; it is a marathon. It is jumping in and saying, "Malnourishment isn't right." We still need better healthcare and nutrition, but we are seeing kids survive. They're not missing school as frequently. They're learning and growing.

We looked at something that was hard and broken, and we put our shoulder into it and discovered how central food is to hope in any given society. Seven years later, we're seeing that it's getting better. There's still a huge mountain of malnourishment to deal with, but we are committed.

I look at the hard places to see the seeds of hope. And then you have to start doing, start acting. This isn't wishful thinking; it's prophetic thinking. I see glimpses of this in Burundi, and I want to see more glimpses of it here in the United States. It's not an easy answer, but when it comes to hope, I'm not looking for easy answers. I'm looking for nourishing ones.

Chicken Adobo, Esteban de los Reyes Style

Bruce Reyes-Chow

Before we get started, if you are here to debate the exact origin of adobo (yes, it comes from five hundred years of Spanish occupation) or if you want to say there is only one right way to make adobo (Need I remind you that the Philippines is made up of seven thousand islands?), hard pass. All you need to know is that adobo has been adapted by the folx from the Philippines and that this salty, sour comfort food will continue to evolve and adapt far into the future.

What I share with you is my best recollection of how my grandfather made his. Because each region is different, there are countless other ways to make it. The ingredients vary depending on the region or what may be in the fridge. Some prefer the sour, while others like the salty; some make it spicy, while others make it sweet. There are those who prefer it dry, while others are all about the sauce. At the end of the day, there really is no right or wrong way to make adobo. Well, I am sure there is, but that's for another day.

Recipe

INGREDIENTS (SERVES 2–4)

Few people actually measure when making adobo. Measurements are, at best, estimates of your heart's desires and memories of love passed down from generation to generation. I measured this time to give you a guide, but over time, you might experiment and make it your own.

2–3 pounds chicken (or pork), preferably thighs and drumsticks with bones and skin still present. (Avoid white meat, which tends to get dry. And if you use drumsticks and thighs, I recommend cutting them in half so the marrow can flavor the sauce.)

1 large white or yellow onion, diced

2 tablespoons pickling spice

2 tablespoons brown sugar

2–3 bay leaves

1 tablespoon sesame oil

1 tablespoon vegetable or olive oil

1 cup vinegar (Datu Puti preferred)

1/2 cup soy sauce (again, Datu Puti)

1/4 cup condensed chicken broth

1 entire bulb of fresh garlic, minced (Yes, you heard me right, I said one ENTIRE BULB! There is no such thing as "too much" garlic. Fight me.)

Optional spice: 1/2 cup or to taste of Pinoy Spice (also Datu Puti)

DIRECTIONS

1. It's really difficult to mess this up, so just go with what feels right and avoid burning down anything but the patriarchy.
2. In a saucepan deep enough for the meat to almost be covered, heat the oils on medium-high heat.
3. When the oil is hot, add pickling spice, bay leaves, and garlic. Sauté just until the garlic starts turning brown.
4. Add onions and cook until just starting to brown on the edges.
5. Add meat and brown it up for about 3–5 minutes.
6. Flip the meat over and add soy sauce, vinegar, broth, and sugar.
7. Stir to mix, and bring to a boil.
8. Once it's boiling, lower the heat to simmer, and cover.
9. Cook for about 30 minutes, returning every 10 minutes to stir/turn the chicken or pork, sample the sauce, and adjust to your liking.
10. When it's done, remove the meat into a serving bowl and boil the liquid for about 10 minutes to get that nice thick heavenly adobo juice. Pour over the chicken, or just do adobo sauce shots. Kidding. Kind of.
    NOTE: I usually do not remove the chicken because I am lazy, but doing this thickens the sauce faster.
11. Get a bowl, scoop out a paddle of rice for the ancestors, top it with a heaping scoop of adobo and juice, pull up a chair, and enjoy!

LITURGY
Before We Begin

Before we begin,
We breathe.
In and out.
In and out.

Before we begin,
We notice.
What is here.
What is not.
What we let go of.
What we welcome in.

Before we begin,
We set our hopes,
Our intentions,
Our prayers.

That on this day,
In this hour,
In this kitchen,
We may be present
To the love and justice
That is.

CHAPTER 4

THE KITCHEN AS A PLACE OF TRANSFORMATION

After we have chosen our menu, gone shopping for the best ingredients our resources allow, and prepared our space, the real work begins. It's time to cook! When we begin the process, we have ingredients. When it is done, we have food. A transformation takes place every time we step into the kitchen to prep food, even if simply to warm something up.

While the trend of taking pictures of food and posting them on social media is often criticized, it makes sense that we would feel a sense of pride when we've created something new from a smattering of disparate ingredients. Cooking can be both an art and a craft. We slice, we season, we bake, we sauté, we stir, we grate—all the while striving for the new dish that awaits us at the end of the process. We hope to honor the ingredients we use and, when we finish the process, to end up somewhere close to wonder. A fluffy omelet, a perfectly cooked steak, or a beautifully arranged salad demonstrates that we began with a variety of elements and ended up in a drastically different place. When we put that plate on the table, we—and others—can feel a sense of awe at the transformation.

FINDING AWE IN THE KITCHEN

Awe is so often undervalued. Our cynical society rarely leaves us with room to feel amazed and inspired. We tend to leave awe as something experienced by children. Perhaps this is why, in the gospel writings, Jesus tells his followers they must become like children to be his disciples. Jesus wanted to be around people who were open to and could experience wonder! Awe requires that we leave our jadedness behind. Awe requires that we see the miraculous in the everyday. Awe also can give us the opportunity to see the possibility of a new way of being. It's often in those moments of awe that we can see a glimpse of the world and our own lives as we hope they could be. The kitchen is a perfect place to practice experiencing such amazement and to let it lead us to creating a more just and generous reality.

Jason Chesnut, a pastor, storyteller, and filmmaker, has spoken about appetite issues. He often does not have a desire to eat, and at times does not feel comfortable eating around other people. One of the ways Jason deals with his struggles is by cooking. Jason's newfound joy in the kitchen is also a discovery of transcendence in watching the elements change. "I had to gather all of the ingredients, like a big scavenger hunt. I like that aspect—gathering all these different elements together. And then when it comes to cooking it, the time it takes to do that, I'm experiencing this food transition. Heat is the main way this happens, obviously, but all aspects of it—when you salt it, when you add acid—when we transform the food, it's like we're living into one of our vocations as human beings." The sense of wonder Jason embodies comes from watching transformation in the kitchen. "Last night, I caramelized some onions. What is more magical than that? I didn't do anything except add heat to onions, and they changed states. It's incredible!" Maybe the same can be true of our lives, our communities, and the world.

A Sourdough Statistic
Derrick's Story

Historians tell us that the invention of bread happened almost simultaneously in different parts of the world at the dawn of the agricultural age. From Asia to Central America, burgeoning civilizations had the same idea to crush the seeds of a grass, mix the powder with water, and bake it into something that not only was edible, but became a staple food item. That in and of itself is astonishing!

My first attempts at bread-making were yeasted breads made with store-bought dried yeast. They were pretty good, but after a few successful attempts, I decided to give sourdough a try. I have to marvel at the genius and adventurousness of early humans. Fermentation is an absolutely brilliant discovery . . . likely made by mistake. That there are "wild yeasts" in the air in my home is disturbing if I think about it for too long, but you can't argue with the results.

After a couple of days, the starter mix of water and flour starts to have little air bubbles in it. The airborne yeast is doing its thing. After a few more days, the mixture starts to bubble over, spewing a buoyant glob onto the kitchen counter. That's usually when you know it's ready. Those wild yeasts from the air in my house then spread throughout the dough mixture and make it rise. Every step of this feels like some ludicrous alchemy, but it works, and it has for thousands of years.

The final product of this magical process is different every time based on how much rest the dough has had, how much I've worked it, how well the yeast has spread, the temperature and humidity of the room, and a seemingly endless number of other factors. In a non-mechanized process, like the one in

(continued)

my kitchen, no two loaves of bread are the same. It feels like an art as well as a science. I've made a few loaves that I have been truly proud of both in terms of look and taste. I don't just marvel at the transformation of water, flour, and salt that takes place in my kitchen. I marvel that this process has sustained human life from the dawn of civilization.

We've written about our kitchens connecting us to family history and cultural history. Bread connects us further, to prehistory. It has for all of human history stood as a symbol of sustenance and provision. That our pre-scientific ancestors mastered a process that has remained virtually unchanged is astounding!

TRANSFORMING SCARCITY TO ENOUGH

For those in Christian tradition, there's one familiar story in the Bible that leads us to awe, a story important enough that all four Gospels included it. For context, even the birth of Jesus wasn't included in all four.

The story goes that Jesus was teaching and was surrounded by a huge crowd. There is the sudden realization, we assume after a few hours of preaching, that the crowd is getting hungry. Jesus's disciples inform him that he might be losing the crowd to growling stomachs and suggest that they call it a day and send folks back to town to get something to eat.

Jesus, in one of his "keep the party going" moods, tells his friends that they should find something for the crowd to eat. Incredulous, the disciples inform Jesus that it would likely take a month's budget to feed every person gathered. Jesus insists. Reluctantly, the disciples scour the gathering, looking for anything that could possibly feed this many people. They find a boy who has two small fish and five loaves of bread and bring him to Jesus. Pleased with his followers' resilience and the boy's generosity, Jesus takes the food, offers thanks for it, breaks it apart, and his friends distribute it to the crowd. Somehow, those tiny fish and a few loaves of bread provide enough food that, even after eating, people are taking home leftovers. Versions of this "transformation of food" can also be found in other traditions, and a familiar children's story, "Stone Soup," speaks to humble beginnings, need, and then wonder and multiplicity.

Among the interpretations of this feeding-of-the-crowds story and its miracle, one that is common imagines that the bread and fish magically regenerate or replicate. That's cool and certainly counts as a miracle, but it doesn't teach us the participation aspect of justice that another view holds, suggesting that what happens here is that seeing the boy blessed for giving up what he had, others in the crowd are moved and decide to give what they have to the cause. What results is a ripple effect of resilience and generosity, so much so that there ends up being more than enough for everyone. Perhaps the real miracle is people learning to be creative and generous with what they have in their possession. Perhaps what is in most need of transformation is not just the foods of our kitchens, but *us*.

This story feels particularly relevant in trying times, whether it's being starkly aware of food insecurity's devastation or holding the reality of the climate emergency and how it affects all of us, but more so communities of color and people of the global majority. In our work we discourage using the term "food desert" and encourage embracing the term "food apartheid" with the recognition that food scarcity isn't some naturally occurring feature in our society. It is a system created by a willingness to unequally distribute food. This Jesus story offers us a road map, a pattern, for how to live transformatively in times of need, and a reminder of how scarcity and abundance are so closely tied with our experience of food.

This feeding story begins with the hunger of the people. Jesus knew that teaching ideas to hungry people was not enough. The people who Jesus fed—and who ultimately fed each other—were gathered to listen to this itinerant man preach. They were the outcasts and economically challenged of their day—people who had no power or influence, but recognized the authenticity of Jesus and the transformation he taught.

It's a story to consider bringing to our kitchens. Paying attention in our kitchens might mean acknowledging the world around us in new ways. Our eyes are being opened to systemic injustice, cracks in the systems, places of struggle and brokenness in the world. We may be learning in a new way about the injustices in our food systems and how there is disproportionate suffering based on race and economics. Jesus saw this and was intentional about hanging out with the crowds who were pushed to the edges of society at the time.

When dinnertime came around on that mountain, the people in the crowd were hungry. Because Jesus was paying attention to what was going on with those around him, he noticed that. He saw their need. The texts say he was moved to "compassion." Or that's how the Greek word used is generally translated, but it's more visceral than that. The word also conveys that Jesus's heart went out to them—his insides, his guts, his very being saw the need on the face of humanity that he loved.

In our kitchens we're called to see the needs and the struggles in our neighborhoods and in our world. We know the kitchen is a place of transformation, and it is a microcosm of understanding how we might be part of a solution.

From a feeding perspective, this multiplicity story invites us to stay aware of the big, global picture, while focusing hyper-locally: What are the needs in our own community, and how can our kitchen be part of transforming scarcity into abundance and healing the broken and struggling places?

While no one of us can individually take on the suffering of the millions of people globally who are hungry right now, we can genuinely show care for Tyron and Linda, Enrico and Dan, and Peter and Rosana, who live in our local community. And we can pay attention to how the stewardship of our own kitchens can have an impact on others. Every one of us is called to do our part. Not everything. Not solve all the problems, but to do our part.

In one of the accounts of the Jesus story, he tells his friends, "You give them something to eat." Essentially, "Feed them yourselves." Then he asks how many loaves of bread they have. They respond, "Five, and two fish"—and a co-creating community forms to create a solution. This situation cuts to the heart of a perpetual internal dialogue many of us have: *Will there be enough food? How will we share with our neighbors? What is it wise and safe for me to do? What is for others to do?*

The answer begins with gathering and bringing what you have. "Bring what you've got." Bring the five loaves of bread, that half-used tub of yogurt, and the tomatoes from your neighbor's backyard. Bring those two fish, the leftover rice from takeout last night, and bring your willingness to be creative.

The "little" we have—the crumbs we have to offer to others—is blessed. The Divine blesses the bread and fish, blesses the loaf and cup, blesses the meal you dropped off at your neighbor's place, and the purchases you made at your local farm to support the livelihood of others. What is blessed is what we perhaps judged as not being enough.

WHAT DO YOU HAVE?

We know we are not alone in feeling like there is not enough in our own kitchens at times. Whether we're struggling with affording to buy food or we haven't had enough time to purchase any, many people can relate to the feeling of opening the refrigerator and saying, "There's nothing to eat." While certainly a lack of food is a stark reality in some kitchens, for other kitchens, it's not as much that there isn't *any* food as it is that there isn't any food that is easy to prepare or that is exciting to contemplate eating.

The story of feeding the crowds offers us a very practical suggestion for where to start: What do you have? is the first question. What is already in your refrigerator and cabinets? What do you find in the pantry? When we look at our food in terms of what we *do* have, rather than what we don't, we may quickly find that we actually have more than we think—and enough to share. When we come from a posture of abundance, rather than scarcity, we find that our creativity starts to grow and we are tossing some sausage in a pan with broccoli and wondering what might happen if we throw a few eggs in.

Now, for the cooks who are exact recipe followers, we acknowledge that this probably sounds like a terrible idea. But maybe even for those of us who would prefer to have all the ingredients exactly lined up, this perspective shift can be a spiritual practice we can take on. As we begin to focus on what we do have, rather than what we don't, might the creative juices start to flow as you respond to your resources rather than to your scarcity?

In the era of "just Google it," one can quickly find all sorts of recipes. One practical practice that we use is to Google the random ingredients we have in our kitchens and see what comes up. Type in "rice, cheese, onions, recipe" and see what appears.

Another way to support yourself to be ready for these creative "there's not enough" moments is to make sure you always have a few basic seasonings and staples available. For our kitchens, that consists of olive oil, salt, pepper, and garlic. Having these basics available helps us improvise with whatever else we have.

Using what we have on hand also relates to leftovers and "repurposing" food. Connie McOsker, a mother of five and a leader at the Garden Church—an urban farm and outdoor sanctuary in San Pedro, California—is the queen of leftovers and repurposed food. Connie's family will all tell you that she is constantly using leftovers in subsequent meals. You'll first see the chicken whole and roasted, and then the next day in a stir fry, and then finally in a soup. Nothing gets wasted, including leftovers many would at first believe are not usable: the chicken bones, the outer dry skin of an onion.

Connie tells stories about how her mother had very little food growing up and had to make do with whatever was there. Connie's mom grew up in a small village in Italy with their food for the year coming from their gardens. They canned their tomato sauce and dried their herbs for winter cooking.

Connie traces the thread of her awareness of food-use to her mother's experience with food as a child. "I believe maybe why I've become so extreme is because of how precious food was for my mom," she reflects, adding that she enjoys this creative transformation of what she has and enjoys teaching food awareness to others too.

Connie has taken this joy to help feed the broader community as well. "I was connected to someone in the community that did the cooking and cleaning after large events. So I would get calls in the middle of the night to come pick up leftover food that would otherwise get thrown away. The cooks and the cleaners were allowed to take some home, but it was just such a large amount that it was offered to me. Then other people started hearing about it. And if there was an event in downtown San Pedro, I got those leftovers too. And then that led to two large freezers in our home, filled with food that could then be shared with those who were hungry in the broader community."

Whatever space we live in, whatever our financial limitations around food, we all have the opportunity to look at what we have and transform it into "enough."

THERE IS ENOUGH

Bruce Reyes-Chow, who shared his Chicken Adobo recipe in chapter 3, talks about how the idea that "there is enough" has become freeing and hopeful for him. While we are transformers in our kitchens, we also can be transformed by our kitchens. Our culture often communicates: "Oh, that's not enough, we've got to do more or have more," Bruce says.

In response he says he has pushed himself and others "to answer the question, What is enough? And that has been really freeing and hopeful for me," Bruce says. "Because somehow, more often than not, I found the courage to answer the question and then live with it." About the question "What is enough?" he says, "Most of the time, we answer that intellectually, but then don't pay attention to it when we reach the point of enough." His process is to ask himself the question, find a response that he's comfortable with, and then live that response forward. "And that's everything from my work hours to how good I need certain things to look. Hope lies in my ability to answer that question for myself: What is enough?"

For some of us achievement-oriented types, this question is perhaps a bit annoying—maybe even aggravating. Yet, what if the kitchen is a place where we, the cooks, can be transformed—a place where whatever our proclivities, they can be gently challenged, and we can have the space to be changed by the process of intentional cooking? What if, even if we want everything we cook to be great, we come to a place where good enough is actually good enough? "Yes, it sucks," he admits, adding, "but it's liberating. . . . I have let more things fail and not worried about it than I've ever done in my entire twenty-six years in this work. There's just certain things that don't actually matter." If we make space for it, the kitchen can be a place where our mindsets can be transformed from ones of scarcity to acceptance of enough and maybe even an appreciation of abundance.

"What's in the Refrigerator?" Dinner
Anna's Story

My spouse calls it one of my superpowers. I just call it "making dinner from what's in the fridge." It seems that for some, the ability to make something out of whatever is there is a normal way of operating, even though I know for others it is a challenge that sits completely outside of their comfort zone.

Recently we were visiting one of my younger brothers and his new wife, and the conversation about cooking came up. We learned that my sister-in-law and my spouse share the experience of looking blankly in the fridge and seeing "nothing," while my brother and I look in and see the possibilities of what could be dinner.

My sister-in-law shared that growing up, her mom would do meal planning for the whole week, then go to the grocery store and get the needed ingredients. My brother and I chuckled; this was so far from how we were raised, the grocery shopping often being about what was on sale while working on a tight budget, and also what was in season in the garden and at the local produce stands. It was fascinating to see how personality related and combined with family history, nurture, and modeling.

We also learned that this was not the first time this conversation had come up in our larger family and that, in fact, my mom had sat around this very table and had this conversation with some of us just months ago as, for my sister-in-law's bridal shower, my mom created a humorous and useful flow chart, encouraging the exploration of what to do when you did or didn't find things in the fridge.

(continued)

CREATIVE MEAL MAKING

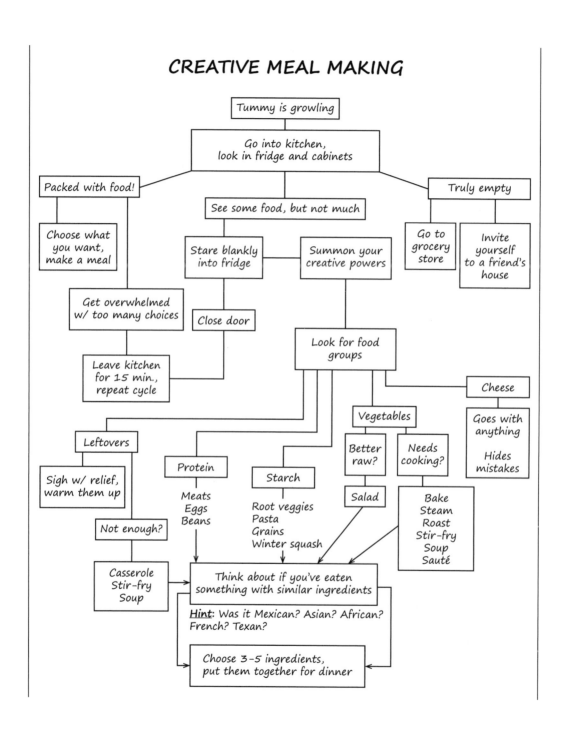

Tummy is growling

Go into kitchen, look in fridge and cabinets

Packed with food! → Choose what you want, make a meal

See some food, but not much

Truly empty → Go to grocery store / Invite yourself to a friend's house

Stare blankly into fridge → Close door

Summon your creative powers → Look for food groups

Get overwhelmed w/ too many choices → Leave kitchen for 15 min., repeat cycle

Cheese → Goes with anything / Hides mistakes

Vegetables → Better raw? / Needs cooking?

Better raw? → Salad

Needs cooking? → Bake / Steam / Roast / Stir-fry / Soup / Sauté

Leftovers → Sigh w/ relief, warm them up → Not enough? → Casserole / Stir-fry / Soup

Protein → Meats / Eggs / Beans

Starch → Root veggies / Pasta / Grains / Winter squash

Think about if you've eaten something with similar ingredients

Hint: Was it Mexican? Asian? African? French? Texan?

Choose 3-5 ingredients, put them together for dinner

This led to several interesting dinnertime conversations in our extended family where we wondered, **Can this skill be learned?** *My husband and my sister-in-law thought, maybe yes, and we've seen and tasted their growing skills at work.*

We got into a fun conversation about how this could maybe even be a fun game or a challenge. I recalled being in a chaplaincy internship years ago where the six of us in the program challenged each other to an evening based on the cooking show **Chopped.** *We started out at the grocery store, each buying another team a set of random ingredients for their assigned part of the meal. We then gathered at the house and took over the kitchen for the next five hours. Two of us made appetizers out of mango, rice paper wrappers, powdered sugar, and peanut butter, while another duo struggled to create a main course with another five obscure ingredients.*

If you, like me, are motivated by challenges, every night can be an episode of **Chopped.** *Your refrigerator will supply the random ingredients, and you and your household will be the judges!*

ENOUGH AND SOME TO SHARE

At the Garden Church, they sing a blessing song each week over the meal:

> There is enough, there is enough, there is enough,
> oh enough, and some to share.

Written by the Rev. Kerri Meyer, these words speak to the call away from scarcity. "There is enough and some to share" was Kerri's heart response to the works of poet Wendell Berry, as well as to her own craving for a life path of abundance. The song weaves together, among other things, words of creation, of loaves and fishes, and of sharing. "The song comes out of the times when I have been without an income, relying on my wife, Jen, and we've only been scraping by in a place where I swear the economy is weighted in favor of the oppression of the Empire," Kerri told us. "I want to be generous, so I have to believe these words. I want to be able to receive generosity, so I have to believe these words: 'There is enough and some to share' is the motto of another possible world."

Kerri Meyer wrote a simple song called "There Is Enough" at a Music that Makes Community workshop, and it quickly became popular. The melody was adapted from a Peter Mayer refrain, and Kerri composed a descant to sing over the tune.

The song is easy to teach or learn together at the table through call-and-response. Simple hand gestures can reinforce the subtle differences between phrases, especially the first and third. Harmony is so intuitive with this song that it may show up even before you invite folks to add it.

The song has been shared in many settings—from a protest in the office of a US senator to church suppers and stewardship campaigns:

There is enough!
There is enough!
There is enough, oh,
Enough and some to share!
Descant: God has blessed her people, God has blessed us!

Rev. Breen Sipes of Tri-Saints Lutheran Parish in rural Nebraska has used additional verses with young people in her community:

I am enough . . .

You are enough . . .

God has enough . . .

While our time in the kitchen is often very personal—we're cooking for ourselves and our households; we are in the kitchen solo or with just a few other people—part of the transformation that happens in a just kitchen comes in the continual reminder that we belong to this bigger world. Practicing transforming "not enough" to "enough and some to share" in our own kitchens is something that flows out from them as well. In fact, these practices facilitate the transformation of possibilities of another way of being in our homes, in our communities, and in our world.

The concept of "another possible world," mentioned by Kerri Meyer above, is one we need right now. We desperately need to open our eyes and our hearts to the needs around us, to let ourselves be moved to compassion for those who don't have enough, to look around and ask: What do we have to offer? How can we collaborate with others? We ask for a blessing on what we offer, and share it freely. And so we move out of the land of hoarding and scarcity and into Jesus's way of multiplicity with the five loaves and two fish, with awe at the abundance right in front of us, and with joy when we truly live believing there is enough, enough and some to share.

WHAT GIVES YOU HOPE?
Kendall Vanderslice

Bread, obviously! And, though it's cheesy, I think sourdough starter is something that really brings me hope. I just started a new one on Saturday, and it's remarkable to me, every time. I can mix together flour, which looks dead and dry and lifeless in the bag. And then I can mix it with water and set it on my counter for three days, and it bubbles back to life. If I keep feeding it, it's just going to grow. And it's going to become more nuanced in its character, in its flavor, in its smell, and in its bacterial profile.

It is a small and tangible reminder that there is life just waiting to spring forth all around us, and that the miraculous is taking place in ways we can't see or don't expect. I can mix the flour and the water together, but there's so much more that happens to bring the world to life. When I see the process that takes place in bread, I'm reminded of my own small-ness in the world and of the mysterious depth of what the Divine is doing. This really gives me hope.

Black Bean Soup

Jason Chesnut

This black bean soup is adapted from the beloved *Moosewood Restaurant Cooks at Home* by the The Moosewood Collective, and it's my go-to when I don't know what else to cook. Cooking this soup centers me.

———————————————— **Recipe** ————————————————

INGREDIENTS

2 16-ounce cans black beans

1 28-ounce can diced tomatoes

1 jalapeño, diced (or 1/4 teaspoon cayenne)

1 teaspoon cumin

2 tablespoon vegetable or canola oil

3 garlic cloves, minced

1 red onion, finely chopped

1/4 cup fresh cilantro, chopped

sour cream, for garnish

DIRECTIONS

1. Set a soup pot over medium heat. Add the oil. Sauté the onions (with a generous pinch of salt), garlic, and jalapeño/cayenne until onions are translucent (about 5 minutes).
2. Next, add cumin, 1/3 cup water, and the can of tomatoes. Cover and bring to a boil.
3. Lower to a simmer, cover, and cook about 5 minutes. Add cans of black beans, cover, and simmer for another 5–10 minutes, stirring occasionally.
4. Remove from heat. Add in sour cream as desired.

LITURGY
Enough

Let "enough" be enough.
Enough time.
Enough food.
Enough you.
And with God,
Maybe there's even
Enough
And some to share.

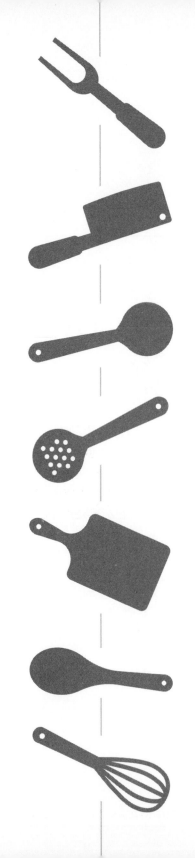

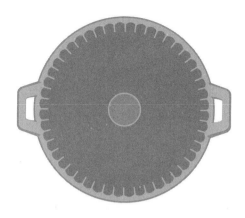

CHAPTER 5

THE KITCHEN AS A PLACE OF REFLECTION

The idea of the kitchen as a place of reflection may sound like utter nonsense to you. Our kitchens are production lines where lunches are assembled. They are chemistry labs with pots boiling over and debris strewn about. They are mad scrambles to the finish line of getting food to the table before our children stage a coup. We may work hard to keep our family and cultural heritage alive in what we serve. We may try to make sure that everything is locally sourced and organically grown. We may try to cook from a place of loving service and mutuality. And on top of all that, we may strive to make the absolute best use of the resources at our disposal. Maybe. Sometimes. And there is still the actual process of cooking: chopping and boiling and seasoning, and watching several burners at a time. There is a delicate dance required to make sure everything hits the plate at the correct temperature and the right amount of doneness. All this while trying to tune out cries of "When will dinner be ready?"

The history of kitchens has been that they work like assembly lines, operating with imbalances of power. Perhaps you feel echoes of this in your very own kitchen. Whereas the production-line kitchen often brings a sense of martyrdom when we start cooking—sacrificing ourselves for the benefit of the community, allowing ourselves to be burned out in the process—the just kitchen is different.

In the just kitchen, the person or people cooking can enjoy the process and maybe even gain new insights and be fed through it. What the just kitchen means is seeing ourselves as deserving of the same care, support, and dignity we long to see for everyone else. Maybe the first question to ask is, What would it look like to turn our kitchen from a frantic space of mindless production into a pleasant space of mindful reflection?

Many think of mindfulness practices or spiritual practices, like praying for others or holding space for others, as part of a structured set of activities that take place in a particular, sometimes "holy" setting. The truth is that many things can be spiritual practices depending on how we approach them. It's less the where than the how. This is something Rev. Dr. Christopher Carter spoke about when he relayed the process of cooking with his young son and his intention to make that time a spiritual practice for both of them. When asked what makes that space a spiritual one, he referred to the mindset in which he approaches the task: "The way that you would know it's a spiritual practice is the posture we take as we participate in it." He recognizes that in order for the experience of cooking to be a formative one for both him and his son, he has to surrender some control. "It's not always going to be the way I think it might be, or how I think it should be, but it's going to be an experience that is shaping me." And part of that experience is storytelling. "Whenever I'm cooking with Isaiah, I'm always talking about what it is we're making, who we're serving, and the places the food, traditions, and recipes came from. If there's a way to connect it to my family, I tell that story."

Mindfulness, in its simplest expression, is about focusing on the present moment instead of ruminating on the past or being anxious for the future. Mindfulness practices invite us to be present with our body, focusing attention on our breath, and allowing thoughts to come and go without chasing after them. It's easy to imagine what mindful eating might look like, and countless books have been written on the subject, encouraging readers to slow down and enjoy the flavors and textures of food, which is good both for digestion and for the overall enjoyment of an eating experience. Adding mindfulness to eating opens the door to having a mindful posture toward other daily activities, giving a greater sense of balance, clarity, and relaxation to life.

So then, what might mindful *cooking* look like? In her thoughtful book *Mindful Thoughts for Cooks: Nourishing Body and Soul*, Julia Ponsonby argues that the way cooking connects us to our senses allows us to connect with our own souls, as well as with the world around us. "When we cook, we are given the opportunity to delight in a whole array not only of tastes, but smells, visual appeal, texture, and sounds. Opportunities for using our senses crop up during the adventure of our meal preparation. . . . This in turn helps us reconnect with and utilize our intuitive and instinctive knowing." Mindful cooking allows us to get out of the habit of moving mechanically through the kitchen in order to manufacture a product, and enables us to fully experience all the tastes, smells, sights, sounds, processes, and experiences that cooking has to offer.

When we can put our attention on our thoughts and feelings, our mind and body, we may find there are things we want to change. Maybe you notice as you are cooking that you often replay the events from the day that made you angry, rehearsing rebuttals while you chop vegetables. Maybe you notice that your annoyance with other household members rises when they interrupt you mid-recipe. When our kitchens become places of reflection, we can become more purposeful about how we engage our thoughts and feelings, and can use our kitchens as places where we can be changed.

In the Christian tradition, there's a Greek word, *metanoia*—it's a word of liberation and change. Literally, it means a "change of mind." Yet the full meaning is more nuanced. It implies making a decision to turn around, face in a new direction, see things differently, see each other differently—to change. Many of the practices and ideas we're exploring in this book are about seeing something differently, about changing our habits and our practices. Not because we will be shamed if we don't buy locally or if we don't compost (well, maybe just a little bit on that one!), but because we truly believe that being changed by the way we engage our kitchens can be part of a bigger change toward the more just and generous world we long for.

Another way of thinking about metanoia is to look at ourselves, our kitchens, and the world around us and ask, What in the kitchen is separating me from the immediate love of whatever my ground of being is—God, the Divine, truth, justice—and from reciprocal love with the people around me?

Part of the work of reflection and change is paying attention to where our food comes from and how the earth and humans and animals were cared for—or not—in bringing it to our kitchen. This reflection and change can also look like noticing the interpersonal dynamics in our households or even within ourselves, and making the changes needed to shift from patterns of injustice to calming practices of equality and care.

There is a creative good in engaging the process of paying attention to what is separating us from each other. When we see it, it's even more inspiring to change our practice, to engage differently, to show up more authentically, to create kitchens where we can consciously choose to engage differently with the world.

For the kitchen to be a space of reflection, one ingredient is crucial: the ability to slow down. Slowing down is hard when we come in from a busy day and immediately throw ourselves into the chore of cooking. Some of what can help us to have more head and heart space in the kitchen is good communication. Letting people know when to expect dinner, or where to find a suitable snack as they wait, can buy a few extra, interruption-free minutes. Extra time can also be created by leaning into the preparation tactics we mentioned in chapter 3.

Of course, there is a difference between having no time and the *feeling* of having no time. Often what needs to slow down in our kitchens is our mind. An anxious mind will make us feel like we have less time than we really have. It will make us think our friends and family are hungry and annoyed while they are perfectly content conversing or playing on their phones. Mindfulness practices help calm our anxious minds and reconnect us with the present moment.

If you are unfamiliar with mindfulness practices, the basics are quite simple, usually centered on the breath. Stop for a minute. Close your eyes and concentrate on your breathing. Feel the air go into your lungs as you inhale and out of your mouth as you exhale. As your mind wanders—and it will—gently bring your attention back to your breath. That refocusing of attention is the practice, coming back to what is real and present as opposed to ruminating about the past or being anxious about the future.

Part of what makes mindfulness such a useful practice is that it reengages our senses and our bodies. Many of us live much of our time in our heads, because of either the work we do or our natural predilections. Author and activist Kelley Nikondeha admits to spending a great deal of time living in the world of her thoughts. Cooking, for her, is one way that she plugs back into the physical world. "I love to read and to write, to play with ideas and constructs, so when I get into the kitchen, it's where I'm able to drop down into my body and into my five senses," she says. "It's the color of the peppers. It's the sound and the rhythm of chopping on a good cutting board with a heavy knife. It's the aromas of the baharat that I put in the rice. . . . It's like my senses come alive and I get outta my head and get into my body." Kelley's observations remind us that a kitchen becomes a just space when those in it have the space and safety to reflect and to fully inhabit their own bodies.

Mindfulness Breath Prayer for Washing Dishes
Breathe in: *Warm water, soap and sponge,*
Breathe out: *a slow rhythm in circles,*
Breathe in: *vessels of transformation*
Breathe out: *ready to nourish again.*

—Christine Valters Paintner

A Few Quiet Moments
Anna's Story

For me, touching base with the land and the soil helps move me from a place of production to a place of intention and reflection—it's often the piece that grounds me to enter the kitchen a little more mindfully. Because I'm a pastor with a busy weekend schedule, Mondays are my regular day off. Which means a day off from my day job, but a day of full-time parenting, as my spouse and I switch off caring for our little one. This past spring, to carve out time for writing this book, we've had the gift of a high school babysitter coming over from across the street for a few hours on Monday afternoons so that I could work on the book and then prepare dinner for our family.

It's been fascinating to pair dedicated time writing about kitchens with spending time in my own. I've become more acutely aware of my experience of cooking and the complexities around it. From working on a chapter about the importance of taking time and space for cooking, to my own rushing into the kitchen to whip up some eggs and sausage to be ready for dinner at 6 p.m., I often find myself jumping right into the tension between the ideals of the just kitchen and the reality of my life. Which is a constant invitation for reflection.

From late spring through the fall, one of my most grounding spiritual practices comes right before the kitchen—harvesting in the garden. Whether it's with my toddler running around and picking all sorts of things, or a quiet solitary trip to the backyard garden, this time of paying attention helps set the scene for the cooking I am about to do. Fresh peas, new lettuce leaves, and fresh herbs go into the colander, and I marvel at the crispness of each leaf and the potency

(continued)

of the flavors. Even if it's just five minutes, it feels like a gift I can give myself to start the cooking process out in the garden.

Once I'm inside, I take solitary kitchen time as a special treat. While there's certainly something joyful about the toddler in her kitchen tower and my husband setting the table, when it's just me in the kitchen, I find it a place to reflect. I can let my mind wander in meandering prayer as the feel of my hand holding the knife and the rhythmic movements of chopping create space for my mind to quiet and my heart to settle. Even when the pace picks up and I'm juggling the potatoes boiling in one pan and the fish braising in another, I find there's something about the rhythm that I can get lost in.

For me, practices in which I can get absorbed and let go of the other thoughts and anxieties that often travel with me are essential to my well-being. When cooking holds some intentionality, it gets me out of my head and into my body—half the battle. And though there is a "product" at the end of it, the process is the practice. And so, by the time we sit down at the table to eat, my soul has already been fed.

COOKING AS SPIRITUAL PRACTICE

Connecting with our bodies in the present moment is one way of making the kitchen a reflective space. But if we are willing, our experience in the kitchen can go from being a mindfulness practice to being a spiritual one.

Kelley Nikondeha doesn't feel her kitchen is just a place of embodiment, but also a place where she can move beyond her body. "I pray there, I remember there. I reflect based on what I am cooking." She talks about how the kitchen brings certain people to mind for her in a prayerful way. Kelley spoke of friends of hers, a young couple, who were moving to Spain for a year to figure out their direction in life. With intentionality, she committed to buying Spanish olive oil for that year. "This way, every time I reached for the olive oil—which was multiple times a day— seeing that Spanish olive oil always brought them to mind." As she put the olive oil in a pan, she thought of them. As she added it to the pesto she was making, she thought of them. "And thinking of them brought me regularly to a one-word or a one-sentence prayer for them." They were kept close to Kelley by making them a part of her daily life—so much of which is lived in the kitchen. "Even today," she said, "every now and then when I grab Spanish olive oil, I still think of them and pray a blessing for them."

MAKING ART IN THE KITCHEN

There are many ways to be reflective. Mindfulness gives us space to reflect on the present moment, the nature of our thoughts, and the experience of our senses. Spiritual practices allow us to reflect on our experience of the Divine and our care for others. Many people we interact with find that cooking allows them to reflect by giving them a space to be creative. Cooking often gives us a chance to make something that is both beautiful to the eye and pleasing to our senses of smell and taste. In fact, cooking is one of the few modes of artistic expression that engage all five of our senses.

And while Chris Carter's experience of the kitchen is as a place of intention to release control, Rev. Bruce Reyes-Chow appreciates the level of control he has in the kitchen and the freedom that control gives him to create. "When I'm in the kitchen, every detail is really important. How I dice onions and what they look like and how the garlic is prepared. Even when I make salsa, how much I roast the ingredients first. I would love to think it is a deeper connection to the food and to my hands and grounding, but it's also just a space that I get to have control over and create in, in a way that I'm not worrying about other people's lenses and views. I just get to create something."

Jason Chesnut, the filmmaker we met previously, has a different mindful intention in the kitchen, a different creative process. As he compares filmmaking with the kitchen experience, he sees similarities in striving to master a craft. "There are plenty of things that I still don't know about editing or filmmaking. I'm constantly learning. There are things I don't know about cooking as well. You just need to try it out and see, and you'll learn more. And for every time I've over-salted something, I've also over-exposed somebody on screen. I get a lot of time to spend with them on the editing-room floor trying to fix those mistakes." As his love for cooking continues to develop, Jason finds himself equally passionate about improving at both of his artforms. "I've experienced this in stories I've heard from Japan, especially the world of ancient Japan, of samurai and others who would spend all day long trying to perfect their craft—whatever that craft was. I've always been inspired by that dedication. I feel like cooking has become that for me, and filmmaking has been that for most of my life. From the minute I picked up a camera, I've always felt like, *How do I do this? How do I continue to learn this? And how do I get better?*"

Khadija James is the owner of a newly launched business called Deez Cookies. She was surprised to find—after a lifetime of thinking of herself as not creative—that baking was an outlet for her imagination. "I can't draw my way out of a paper bag. My children ask me to help them with their little drawings. And I reply, 'It's gonna be just as good if you do it yourself.' But I have learned through cookies that I am creative. And that has been an unexpected gift." Her creativity comes out in unique flavor combinations based on themes she finds important. "My Women's History Month box is a shout-out to Captain Planet/Gaia. It is earth, fire, wind, and heart. I skipped water because blue cookies are hard. But my fire cookies are actually named for a Black female pitmaster in rural Tennessee. Her name is Helen Turner. And she uses hickory and oak wood, not charcoal. She's literally tending fire while making sides and working the front counter. This lady is incredible. But the shortbread has a dry rub that I've designed—some tomato powder, some oak-based syrup, oak smoke, and hickory smoke syrup. So it tastes like barbecue. Like, wow. Almost like a good barbecue potato chip. Like a potato chip meets bread. So it's delicious, but it's also the most bizarre experience!" Khadija's work illustrates how our kitchens need not simply be spaces of production, but instead can become laboratories for innovation, mindfulness, intention, and creativity. When we allow ourselves room to breathe and space to play, we open the door for inspiration, insight, and new paths forward.

A Recipe Is Just a Suggestion
Derrick's Story

Before the pandemic, my wife loved to cook. The kitchen was a reflective space for her, a space to shift gears from her full-time work as a pastor to her other full-time work of being a wife and a mother. With the pandemic, she began working from home, and the work/life boundary became something of a blur. At various points in the first year of the pandemic, there were as many as six of us in the house, needing food three times a day before we all went to our separate spaces. It became more essential for me to share the cooking responsibilities. I was happy to do it! Of course, taking on additional responsibility is as good an excuse as any to buy new books. Like many people who were rediscovering their kitchens during lockdowns, I purchased Samin Nosrat's book **Salt, Fat, Acid, Heat: Mastering the Elements of Good Cooking.** *On one hand, I wanted the recipes the book had to offer, but I was more interested in the foundational premise of the book: that cooking could be reduced to these four elements, and that combining them in the right proportions could make any meal a winner. The goal for me was to gain that ability that all great chefs and home cooks seem to have—being able to grab random ingredients from the refrigerator and cabinet and make something delicious without a recipe, just with the intrinsic knowledge of what tastes good.*

I appreciate a good recipe. But if cooking is a creative endeavor, then cooking with a recipe sometimes feels like paint-by-numbers. Sure, you might get slight variations from what the original artist intended, but ultimately, you are using their paintbrush and not your own. Recipes, in my mind, can sometimes stifle creativity in the kitchen.

I've rarely ever followed a recipe to the letter. Even when I am baking bread, which demands a certain level of precision, I'll usually add a few more grams of salt than what is called for. When I cook, I want everything I make to have a little bit of my fingerprint on it (not literal fingerprints—usually).

The kitchen is a great place to experiment! We should try new things. We should push our palates. We should create new flavor combinations. We should explore spices and seasonings from outside of our own culture. And we should be willing to fail from time to time. A failure in the kitchen isn't the worst thing in the world. Very few of my kitchen failures have been totally inedible. And the few that were? Well, that's what DoorDash is for!

KITCHEN DEBRIEF

Nora Woofenden, Anna's younger sister, and Nora's housemate Harshita Bhargava have offered a beautiful example of how their shared roommate kitchen provides a place for reflection and supports the work of justice. While they lived together, there were four housemates in graduate school for various therapist programs.

Each of the four in their own way worked with the injustices in the mental health world, while navigating being a new professional in that field. They were busy! Their schedules were full. But it was in the kitchen, Nora said, "where we would come together and we would cross paths. If someone was cooking, then someone else would come out and make a cup of tea and talk through our day. So the kitchen got to be that hub and that communal space where we were talking through the world and our interaction with it." All four of them shared this feeling of having found the kitchen to be a place where they all could resource—body and soul—and have deep conversation, a place where they could support each other in their calls to "treat individuals and the world with care and justice."

It's unlikely that we can completely overcome the notion of cooking as a chore. Every day we have to come up with three meals (ideally) for at least ourselves. Maybe it's inevitable that it would feel like a grind. What we hope is that by providing ideas for a just kitchen, we all can move cooking from being a chore to being a ritual. Rituals imbue routines with meaning and opportunities for reflection. We believe that if we set that as an intention, cooking can be a ritual that makes space for mindfulness, metanoia-change, and creativity. And just as the rituals of our spiritual communities offer healing to our spirits, perhaps in our kitchens the ritual of cooking can begin to bring healing to our bodies and minds.

Mindfulness Basics: Five Commonly Held Mindfulness Practices

1. *Nonjudgmental.* Be an impartial witness to your own experience. Become aware of the constant stream of judging and reacting to inner and outer experience.

2. *Beginner's mind.* Remaining open and curious allows us to be receptive to new possibilities and prevents us from getting stuck in the rut of our own expertise.

3. *Non-striving.* The goal is to be with yourself right here, right now. Pay attention to what is unfolding, without trying to change anything.

4. *Acceptance.* See things as they are. This sets the stage for acting appropriately in your life no matter what is happening.

5. *Letting go.* When we pay attention to our inner experience, we discover there are certain thoughts, emotions, and situations the mind wants to hold onto. Let your experience be what it is right now.

Pomegranate Salad

Kelley Nikondeha

This is a salad that was inspired by a friend in Jerusalem and embellished with flavors from my time in the Old City. The pomegranates and oranges piled high at fresh-fruit stands and juiced into a cup before my eyes are a favorite culinary memory I recreate with that combination in this salad.

Recipe

INGREDIENTS

1 1/2 cups cooked grain (barley, farro, or even a couscous could work)

2 tablespoons pomegranate molasses

3 tablespoons olive oil

2 tablespoons red wine vinegar (though a citrus vinegar is a nice option too)

1–2 oranges' worth of zest (and juice, if you like extra zing)

1 cup chopped mint

1 cup chopped parsley

1 cup roughly chopped walnuts

1 cup roughly chopped hazelnuts

1 cup pomegranate seeds

salt and pepper to taste

DIRECTIONS

1. To the cooked grain (I most often use barley), add vinaigrette made of pomegranate molasses, vinegar, olive oil, and salt and pepper. Make it to your taste; the measurements are just a suggestion here.

2. Add in the zest of an orange; you can add the juice if you want more citrus zing. Add copious amounts of mint and parsley. Add in handfuls of walnuts and hazelnuts—they will be more flavorful if you toast them first, but sometimes there isn't time, and that is still all right. Add pomegranate seeds, and season with salt and pepper to taste.

3. Mix together and you have a salad that is beautiful, healthy, and addictive.

4. The secret of this recipe is that none of the measurements are fixed. It is all to taste—how tart you want your vinaigrette, how well dressed you want the grains, if you want more walnuts than hazelnuts. It's all up to you. Sometimes I top with orange supremes and an extra drizzle of pomegranate molasses.

LITURGY
Attention

Deep breath,
And release.

Attention
On the lettuce,
Each water droplet,
As it falls off the leaf.

Attention
On the chicken,
Thighs and skin,
Seasoned and placed
In the pan.

Attention
On the potatoes,
As the twirls of skin
Roll off the peeler
And into the compost.

Attention
On the parsley,
And thyme,
And sage.
Stop
And rub them
Between your hands
Take your hands
To your face,
And breathe in.
And out.

Attention.

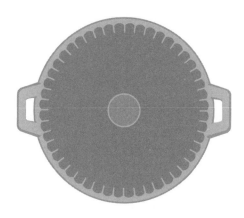

CHAPTER 6

THE KITCHEN AS A PLACE OF HEALING

It wasn't until 1994 that nutrition labels became mandatory for most food products. This was the culmination of a decades-long shift as the public began to demand more accountability for what corporations put into consumable products. It was believed that putting health information on food would make people eat healthier and thus have better medical outcomes. While that happened to some extent, an unexpected result was a rapid rise in diet-based diseases coupled with wave after wave of fad diets, each claiming the correct nutritional balance. Where there seems to be growing consensus is that diet-related illnesses such as diabetes and hypertension are deeply connected to hyper-processed foods that contain large amounts of salt and sugar in various chemical forms.

The intent of putting nutritional content on our foods was admirable. It came from a belief that (1) we should know what is being put into our bodies and (2) what we eat can help heal our bodies—or contribute to their slow poisoning. A just kitchen can be a place where we get in touch with what our bodies need so that as we heal, we can be a healing presence in the world.

Isabel Ramirez-Burnett, a certified health and wellness coach originally from the Dominican Republic, experienced the kind of harm that can be caused to the body by the foods we eat. She spoke with us about how her move from the Dominican Republic to the United States brought a shift in her perspective on food. In the Dominican Republic, she grew up learning to cook. "We had a farm, we had a lot of animals, we had a large vegetable garden, we got everything we needed for the week. So cooking from scratch and cooking fresh food has just been a part of my upbringing." When she moved to the States, at first she embraced the convenience of not having to prepare foods from scratch. "I bought into believing that this is what developed nations do, and it is great! You can just go to the supermarket and get what you want easily and go through the drive-thru and get whatever you want and not have to cook it." But after several years of this eating pattern, chronic illnesses caught up to her. "I had to realize what I was doing differently in the Dominican Republic and what I was doing now that was having such a bad influence on me," she reflected. "And food was a huge part of that."

Much of the journey Isabel embarked on of healing from those chronic illnesses began in her kitchen. That meant reconnecting with foods and cooking styles from the Dominican Republic. Now in her kitchen, she says, you will find "what we call *adobo* and *sofrito*, which is a way that you can make pretty much every meat and vegetable. My family absolutely loves Dominican beef, which is just beef cooked in that style. And root vegetables, which are something that I had disconnected from for a while—plantains and yucca and other root vegetables that are less common in the States, but that you can get in Hispanic stores. These are frequently found in my kitchen."

Isabel's personal journey led her into a career where she helps others use food as a significant part of their healing. "I was lucky enough to have a doctor who did admit that food had some influence. And then for the next fifteen years, it was just a journey of experimenting with food, reading a lot of books, going back into my roots, and trying to incorporate that more and more. The constant was that I knew that when I paid very close attention to what I ate and stayed toward the healthy end, I did feel better. I would cook a lot and post on Facebook, and people would ask me about it. And I enjoyed it! I enjoy being able to say to someone, 'This is what I'm doing . . .' and having someone come back to me and say, 'I tried that, and it really worked.' My desire is to help people really know what causes chronic illness." Isabel's deep belief that her own kitchen can be a place of healing led her into teaching others how to find healing in theirs.

We first connected with Isabel through our friends at the *Death in the Garden* podcast. Both Jake and Maren also had stories of their health being impacted by dietary choices. Maren, in particular, was very open about the need to heal her relationship with food after dealing with eating disorders. While taking up rock-climbing helped her change her disordered behavior around food, it didn't heal her relationship with food. What actually became part of that healing was her cooking—specifically, cooking more animal-based products that she had previously avoided. "I feel like recently it's become much more of a devotional thing. This food makes me feel so satiated and so grateful, and all of these things I'm still working out, like healing from my past, healing from the sort of dynamics that I had with food, are slowly gaining healing and attention." Maren credits learning how to cook meat not just with her ability to move beyond her eating disorders but with changing her perspective on food. "I was actually pretty vegetarian when I was in college, purely out of just not knowing how to cook meat or the health issues. But now, eating steaks and eating beef and eggs and cheese and all of those things, I'm developing such a better relationship with food." Her healing journey with food isn't everyone's journey, but the just kitchen is about each of us, in our unique ways, finding a better relationship with our body and the foods we bring into our kitchen for the sake of our own healing and the healing of others.

COOKING AS HEALING

Healing in the kitchen isn't only about what is being cooked, but also about the act of cooking itself. Jason Chesnut, who was introduced earlier, has spoken about his immense struggles with anxiety. Oftentimes that anxiety causes him to lose his appetite for long periods of time. Yet in 2020, he suddenly became incredibly passionate about cooking, and cooking became a part of his healing process. "Even just doing food prep sometimes opens up my appetite. I never take for granted the sense of feeling hungry and then being sated and energized or rested—or whatever you feel after you eat." Even when his appetite doesn't return to him, Jason finds that the act of cooking can be a balm for his anxious mind. "When I've scheduled out time to be in the kitchen, even if I don't eat, my stress and anxiety go down, which is probably why I'm eating more inside my own kitchen. I just feel like there's something sacred going on there."

Eating My Feelings
Derrick's Story

Food is deeply connected to our mental health. Some of us eat when we're sad. Some of us can't eat when we're sad. Sometimes we let the feeling of hunger override all of our other feelings. Sometimes we push down hunger as much as we do anger or fear. We designate certain foods as "comfort foods"—and very few of us choose carrots as our comfort food.

For me, 2014 was a particularly hard year. I went through a difficult divorce and had major professional setbacks, all consequences of my own actions. I worked a retail job that kept me on my feet all day, which was exhausting, and I wasn't making much money. My weight plummeted. While it was nice to see my abs again, I knew I wasn't healthy. There were times when I was just too sad to eat, or I wouldn't eat because I hate eating alone. At that point in my life, food was just an expense, not a joy.

Fast-forward a year, and I was in a new job in a new city. The pendulum on my eating swung to the other extreme. Eating became the thing I did whenever my mind or hands were idle. I vividly remember sitting down to watch television one afternoon and the sadness of the previous years washing over me. Instead of sitting with those feelings or talking them out with someone, I immediately ran to the kitchen and grabbed chips and salsa. My weight skyrocketed. Once again, for different reasons, I wasn't in the healthiest spot. I was eating my emotions instead of feeling and confronting them.

Food has many connections: need, comfort, escape, our own emotional history, and also celebration. Food can be so deeply ingrained into the idea of celebration that we don't know how to celebrate without it or without eating to

(continued)

excess. As much as we eat both for and against nutrition and physical health, we also eat both for and against our mental health.

Cooking is no substitute for therapy, a strong support system, or medication if mental health issues warrant, but my own relationship to food and the emotions associated with it changed significantly once I started spending time in the kitchen in ways that went beyond merely heating up a can of soup or warming a frozen pizza. When I cook, I overeat less. The pace of cooking often gives me space to sit with harder emotions while also doing something productive for myself and my family. And I have a greater overall appreciation for food because I've spent more time with it in the kitchen. That appreciation makes me less likely to use food as an emotional crutch.

Our relationships with food can be incredibly complicated. During the process of writing this book, hearing people's willingness to share about eating disorders, food addictions, and connections between food and trauma in their lives has shifted understandings for me. There's no blanket cure for these issues, yet the acts of sourcing, preparing, and cooking food hold possibilities for the beginning of a healing process for many. In positive and meaningful ways, spending time in the kitchen, with attention, changes our relationship to food.

LETTING GO OF OLD STORIES
IN OUR KITCHENS

We've looked, in part, at some of the long histories of injustice and abused power connected with our food systems. Our kitchens, we believe, can be places where we begin to push back against those injustices and start to heal broken systems as well as our personal traumas. At the start of this book, we looked at the ways cooking often has a power dynamic attached to it: people without power cook for those who have power. For many, the way to heal from these systems of oppression has been to leave the kitchen altogether. But as some have reflected further on that dynamic and have returned to the kitchen, they have found that "owning" the space and cooking with intention for the sake of healing have given them back the kitchen spaces that have felt stolen from them.

In the introduction to her 2021 essay collection, *Why We Cook: Women on Food, Identity, and Connection*, Lindsay Gardner outlines the story of inequality in the kitchen related to the lives of women. Citing a 2018 study, she points to the fact that women spend on average fifty minutes a day cooking, whereas men on average spend only twenty minutes. She also cites a 2017 study that reveals that while a large percentage of the food service industry is made up of women, only 24 percent of head chefs in restaurants were women as of the time of that study. In her collection of interviews with over one hundred women in the food industry, Gardner's intention is not just to highlight these inequities, but to allow space for women's stories to instigate a process of understanding. "In sharing their stories they expand our collective understanding of the complex, nuanced relationships women have with food and cooking." Their voices, gained as they pushed against the imbalance of power, "reveal the power of food to sustain, uplift and nourish, channel joy, and effect change."

Nikki Cooley, of the Diné (Navajo) Nation, resides in northern Arizona. She is of the Towering House Clan, born for the Reed People Clan, and her maternal grandparents are of the Water That Flows Together Clan, with her paternal grandparents of the Manygoats Clan. As Nikki was growing up, her kitchen experience was intergenerational—the whole family was present and participated in jobs and chores around, for, and within the kitchen.

While each family, community, and group is different, Nikki's experience was that the matriarchs were in charge of the kitchen, even as the men, women, and children were all part of the food preparation and cooking. "I've been to some kitchens where it's all women. And there is a very clear line that men don't go in there—not because they're not allowed; it's because they don't want to, or have been taught that space is not for them. Or that kitchen work is women's work. But I have never seen that in my family. Yes, you'll see a large number of women and children in the cooking area. But men are asked to take care of specific tasks." This division, or lack thereof, she said, is "indicative of how a family was taught and what rules started getting passed along that it's only women in the kitchen." She acknowledged that these perspectives likely do exist in her own family. "But I give them a hard time for it—things are changing! And we shouldn't say those kinds of things anymore, especially in front of our young children. This space, every space, should be *everyone's* space."

Similarly, much is being written about the African American contribution to regional and national cooking. Understanding that much of this happened involuntarily during enslavement, many are finding their way back to the roots of Black cooking and are celebrating the ways in which agricultural acumen and culinary improvisation of Black chefs can be empowering today. Authors like Michael Twitty, Adrian Miller, Dr. Jessica B. Harris, and Psyche Williams-Forson, to name a few, are helping contemporary Black people find a measure of healing from historical trauma in their kitchens.

In our interview with Dr. Christopher Carter, he discussed the ways a reexamination of soul food is easing the burden of a hard past. "Soul food, at its core, is food that is cooked by Black folks with the kind of ancestral and culinary wisdom that has been passed down to us. It is about the preservation and promotion of the Black community. It's a way in which we can tell our story through our own means and our lens as Black people. Soul food is fundamentally anti-racist because it is a claiming of our story outside of the structures of white supremacy." Chris's understanding of soul food provides a necessary counternarrative to the idea that those who were enslaved somehow were "unskilled" laborers needing purpose and guidance. "The importance of preserving this term, 'soul food,' is because as Black people, it's important for us to remember that we come from an agricultural people—people who were enslaved *because* of our agricultural acumen, *because* of our culinary acumen. Food allows us to recognize this kind of connection that we have." Understanding this history and continuing to tell these stories in our own kitchens, Chris believes, is a part of reclaiming and preserving dignity in the Black community. "It changes the conversation in ways that allow us to assert our own humanness, which is fundamentally crucial. And it gives us the tools we need to heal from these wounds." Chris and others provide both language and inspiration for the kitchen as a place where dignity is restored and deep racial wounds can begin to heal.

HEALING OUR RELATIONSHIP TO CREATION

In the first of two creation stories in Genesis in the Hebrew Scriptures, God declares different elements of the creation "good" after they are brought into existence. Land? Good. Water? Good. Sun, moon, and stars? Good. Plants and animals? Good. But when God creates humans, the language changes. After that sixth day, God looks at the state of things and declares it "very good." While in our human-centric way of interpreting ancient texts, we often read the text as saying that humans are the very good part, the text offers something else. It reads, "God saw everything that God had made, and indeed, it was very good." As our friend John Creasy pointed out, it's not humans that make it very good; it's humans being in right relationship with the rest of creation that is very-goodness.

In chapter 2, we looked at some of the ways our food system distorts a just relationship with creation. We tend to designate nonhuman creation as "nature," something separate from us. But we're clearly a part of the creation narrative, clearly a part of creation itself. By othering nature, we exploit nature. We've depleted the soil, poisoned the water, and polluted the air in the name of an industrial food system, refusing to claim our intrinsic part in those systems.

But healing is possible, according to film producer James Connolly. In his documentary *Sacred Cow: The Nutritional, Environmental, and Ethical Case for Better Meat*, a title we admit might be stomach-churning for our vegan and vegetarian friends, he offers a message that we think will resonate. In the film he advocates for better agricultural practices, often referred to as "regenerative agriculture." Regenerative agriculture works in harmony with nature, resulting in healthier plants, animals, and environments. While animal waste at the level produced by industrial agriculture can be toxic, the lower level of waste of ruminant animals like cattle can actually replenish the nutrients farming takes out of the soil. When those animals are allowed to roam in ways that prevent overgrazing, they add health to the overall ecosystem. What makes this system work is not having more animals on the land than the land can support but, rather, leaning toward smaller, less industrialized operations. The same is true of crops grown in a rotational system. The cycle of bringing foods into our kitchens that have been grown and raised this way brings health to our own bodies because the plants and animals have healthier growing and grazing environments. A rotational system also supports and encourages food production that can be healing to the environment.

Connolly reflects on how animals often get vilified for a system that works perfectly well in nature and when part of a balanced ecosystem. "There is actually a circular system that works in nature. It works for giraffes, it works for wildebeests, it works for moose, it works for reindeer, and it works for cows and sheep and goats and all these other ruminant animals. So why are we blaming animals for a system that we say is environmentally damaging? It just doesn't make sense."

Another documentary film, *Gather*, focuses on Native Americans reclaiming food sovereignty by reclaiming their ancestors' agricultural practices. While it is great to see more emphasis placed on regenerative agriculture practices, we also recognize that much of what is labeled "regenerative" is food grown using Indigenous practices repackaged for modern audiences. Notably, *Gather* also shows a tribal community healing from diseases caused by a Western diet and processed foods, as tribal communities eat in ways more aligned with how their ancestors did.

As one set of communities restores food practices that are ancient and regenerative, we know that most in the United States consume processed and ultra-processed foods. Why? They are convenient, ubiquitous, and big business. Heavily processed food is shelf-stable for a longer time, meaning it is more likely to sell. Heavily processed food also tends to have larger amounts of sugar, salt, and fat—things our bodies crave and to which we can become addicted—meaning that more of this food is consumed to feed the addiction, and more demand is created for sales.

Heavily processed foods are often inexpensive, meaning you can stock up on them, worry less about them going bad, and maybe save a few bucks. Heavily processed foods are often incredibly convenient, either ready to eat from the package or requiring only the addition of heat or water before consuming.

Oftentimes it is the convenience we are paying for—as heavily processed foods are *everywhere*—not just in grocery stores, but gas stations, department stores, restaurants, and vending machines. *Everywhere.*

Most of us have some level of processed food in our kitchens, even though food writer Michael Pollan insists that a just kitchen should contain no processed foods. In his small volume *Food Rules: An Eater's Manual*, Pollan enumerates a list of guidelines: eat actual food, mostly plants, and not too much. Pollan defines what "food" is and how to differentiate it from "food-like substances," which are what he calls processed foods. Food, he says, doesn't have ingredients a third-grader couldn't pronounce. Food doesn't contain high-fructose corn syrup. Food doesn't have more than five ingredients. Food can be traced back to its original state in nature. (In chapter 2, we shared more of this list.)

Pollan's rules aren't wrong. And a person or family eating as he describes would likely be very healthy. However, he assumes a certain level of privilege that not every household has. It's hard to feed a large family by only shopping at a farmers' market. It's unreasonable to think that two busy working adults wouldn't have some quick meals available for those nights when they just can't cook or stop by a grocery store that sells locally sourced food. Lots of people have to leave their neighborhoods to find a grocery store with good meats and vegetables. And communities of color are among the most underresourced in terms of local foods, requiring residents to travel farther for these foods than those in predominantly white communities. Some have called this situation a "food desert," but we've been encouraged to use the term "food apartheid," as this is a created system of racial harm, not "simply" an unexpected lack. While deserts occur naturally, the systems that keep healthy foods within reach of some and out of reach for others are human constructions. We also choose to use this wording because "food desert" is a research term imposed upon communities, whereas "food apartheid" was adopted by the communities that are being described and was popularized by former Black Urban Growers (BUGs) director Karen Washington.

Food Apartheid

"What I would rather say instead of 'food desert' is 'food apartheid,' because 'food apartheid' looks at the whole food system, along with race, geography, faith, and economics. You say 'food apartheid' and you get to the root cause of some of the problems around the food system. It brings in hunger and poverty. It brings us to the more important question: What are some of the social inequalities that you see, and what are you doing to erase some of the injustices?"—Karen Washington, founder of Black Urban Growers (BUGs)

Yes, Pollan's rules are good guidelines. We should strive to have the highest-quality foods in our kitchens that we can afford. When we have the resources, we should be willing to sacrifice a little bit of convenience. But a just kitchen is also a kitchen free of both judgment and shame. We can't expect those of us who don't have the resources of time, money, knowledge, or access to be making the same decisions that people with those resources do, or decisions that we feel are somehow "right." Nor should we allow ourselves to sink into despair when we have to make hard choices between managing the food budget and paying medical bills. In a just world, good food—the way Michael Pollan defines "food"—would be easily accessible to all, and that's something we want to strive for in our world. In the meantime, we should look for ways that work for us, our families, and our communities, taking incremental steps toward the healing of our bodies and the healing of our world.

HEALING TOGETHER

We all have areas of our lives where we need healing. Sometimes the healing we long for is not the healing that is possible, and other times we are surprised by how we are healed in areas we didn't even know were a struggle for us. While maybe only some of us would identify our need for healing as having a direct tie to food, most of us don't need much time to think of a hurt, a wound, somewhere we're stuck, or something that's not working for us that we would like to be healed. And whether the kitchen or food is the primary location of our woundedness, we know there's something about the kitchen that can be part of all our healing.

Whether the healing that is needed is spiritual, emotional, or physical, whether it's personal or involves unresolved conflict or a call for reconciliation among people, God, and the planet, we have found that the kitchen can offer an invitation to the journey of healing.

The gospel writings include many stories of Jesus healing people. Take, for example, Bartimaeus, a man who was blind. He heard that Jesus, the rabbi, was near—the one who reached out across barriers to eat with and teach and touch and heal all sorts of people his tradition forbade him to come into contact with. But Bartimaeus was unable to get to the healer amid the throngs of people, so he called for help, "Have mercy on me!" Bartimaeus's story points out that sometimes our first step on a healing journey is knowing that we want to be healed.

And in another healing story of Jesus in the Gospels, his question goes to the root of things. You can almost hear the words echoing off the walls, running in the water that cleans the root vegetables you bought from a local farm, a question the kitchen asks of us: "Do you want to be made well?" In the previous chapter we talked about the kitchen as a place of reflection. Finding space to reflect can be the beginning of healing, as we ask ourselves if we are actually ready to be well, as we open ourselves up to the desire to have our minds changed and our habits shifted. At times this is a solo effort, but often both our wounds and our healing involve other people.

Looking again at the story of Bartimaeus regaining his sight, we note that the healing takes place within a crowd of people who play a role in the story as well. When Bartimaeus first cries out, the crowd is not on his side. It doesn't take much imagination for us to place this blind beggar on the side of the road in the context of our current communities—an outcast, untouchable, likely uncared for, and literally pushed to the side of the road where he was found begging. Maybe you've been in that place in your own journey of healing, feeling like you're alone and no one understands what you are going through. When Bartimaeus calls out the first time, the crowd tries to shut him up. "Hush, blind man, don't get in the way, and don't disturb the rabbi." But he persists; he won't be silenced for the sake of the crowd's social comfort.

He calls out again for help, for mercy. And then Jesus stands still. In the middle of the noise, the rabbi stops, listens to the call, and meets the man on the margins, in his need. When he does so, something shifts in the crowd. Something changes in them when Jesus stands still and listens to the cry for help. They, too, turn to pay attention, maybe realizing their own need for healing help.

People now turn to Bartimaeus, saying, "Take heart: Get up! Jesus is calling you." Other translations say, "Cheer up!" And one scholar says that "Have courage!" might be a closer wording. This person who was being ignored and even shunned is now surrounded by a crowd of people who are cheering him on and saying, "Have courage! You are not alone!"

We live busy, crowded lives, and something calling for healing wells up within us. We wonder if our kitchens can be the space for our healing journey. Even as we are embedded within all of society and community, and aware of all the people we're connected with for good and for ill, our kitchens can be the place for moments of paying attention, and in those moments we may find healing.

In the process of working on this book and soaking in the stories of others in their kitchens, we have been touched by the way those stories have changed us and continue to call us forward into our own healing. Be it an experience we can relate to because we've gone through something similar, or having our hearts opened up to experiences beyond our own, we find that drawing on the greater community is a powerful part of our healing processes.

As we share the stories in this book, we hope that by being honest with ourselves and one another about our struggles and our practices, it's clear that the invitation to healing is available for all of us. When we read about Jason and his journey into the kitchen, where he meets his own story, his own need, and the way that preparing food becomes a source of healing good; when we listen to Derrick share about his desolate time after a divorce and the wide pendulum swings around food and grief, and how the kitchen became both source and healing; when we read about Anna wrestling with gender roles and finding a place of peace in the power dynamics of her own kitchen, we hope you hear for your own journey, in your own kitchen, voices now gathering as a crowd shouting out, "Have courage! Take heart! You are not alone."

Berengena Guisada (Stewed Eggplant)

Isabel Ramirez-Burnett

When we asked Isabel for a recipe, she was immediately excited to share this eggplant dish from her grandmother. She said it was the recipe all her high school friends used to love. Isabel thanks her grandmother every time she makes it.

—— Recipe ——

INGREDIENTS

2–3 large eggplants

3 cloves garlic

3 tablespoons olive oil

1 medium diced red onion

1 large diced bell pepper

2 cups diced plum tomatoes

1 tablespoon tomato paste

1 tablespoon vinegar

salt and pepper to taste

1 teaspoon oregano

1 teaspoon dried cilantro

1 1/2 cups water

DIRECTIONS

1. Peel and dice eggplant, or for a softer consistency, bake the eggplant ahead of time, then peel and pulse in a food processor. In a frying pan, heat the olive oil, add the onions, and cook until soft. Add peppers and garlic and cook for about 2 minutes on medium heat. Add the tomato paste and mix in, then add the vinegar and deglaze.

2. Add the diced eggplant and brown slightly; if using eggplant from the food processor, just mix in. Add the plum tomatoes, herbs, and water, and bring to a boil. Then lower heat and cook until diced eggplant is soft or until water is mostly incorporated as a sauce. The final result should be eggplant in sauce; you can add more water or stock if it dries out.

3. Taste and adjust seasoning accordingly. You can add leftover meats to the mix if you prefer. Our favorite way to serve this is over rice with beans and avocado and to eat the leftovers cold over bread.

Healing Questions to Bring to Our Kitchens

1. How can I heal my relationship with food?

2. How can food help me heal my relationship with my body?

3. What damaging stories from the past can be healed in the kitchen?

4. How can what happens in my kitchen help to heal creation?

5. How does my healing make the world more just?

LITURGY
Be Healed

It's not as simple as
Just reaching out our hand for help,
Most of the time.
But sometimes,
Maybe often even,
It starts there.

With a simple action.
A choice.
A direction.

That first step
In the journey of
Healing.

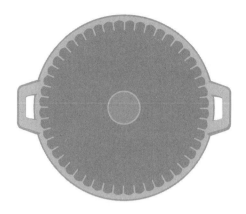

CHAPTER 7

THE KITCHEN AS A PLACE OF COMMUNITY

Many of us, even if we put great attention into creating a welcoming atmosphere in our living rooms—having comfy couches and nice coffee tables—when we have a party or even on a weekday after school, find that family or community who gather actually are drawn instead to the kitchen. The kitchen is a place to interact with one another, opening up lines of connection and communication that come naturally, as someone chops and another stirs.

In this chapter we'll talk about how a just kitchen is a place where people can connect in a unique and healing way, and about the benefits and challenges that come when we cook with others. We'll explore practices to support that work—looking specifically at cooking with children, cooking with a partner or spouse, and cooking as a single person—and how to cultivate community by inviting others into our kitchen.

"GET OUT OF MY KITCHEN!"

Someone has likely said this to you; it's also very possible that you have said it to someone else. So let's be honest: sometimes it's a nuisance to have someone else in the kitchen with you. It's easier to not have to communicate how you want something done and to not feel like you're bumping into each other every three seconds. Sometimes the kitchen isn't big enough for more than one body to maneuver without incident. And sometimes the kitchen is "our" alone space. We get that.

And yet, cooking with others can be incredibly rewarding. It can be educational. It can be romantic. It can also be hilarious. Cooking with someone is just as intimate as eating with them—sometimes more so! Learning how to share space, balance preferences, and assign tasks is a delicate dance. It can also be a lot of fun. When you cook with someone, or a group of someones, a community forms. It's a community built around a common task and shared goals. It can also be built around shared history and culture.

In this chapter we will explore ways we can have community in our kitchen. We'll also discuss how engaging in our kitchens can strengthen communities. And because it often gets overlooked when we think about what "community" means, we will also look at what it's like to cook for a community of one.

COOKING IN COMMUNITY

Most books on food and cooking have changed since the COVID-19 pandemic in terms of the thinking about both. Food and kitchen conversations have changed. People we have talked to were deeply impacted in one way or another by the many pivots required to make our way through the new reality of separation, anxiety, and existential unknowns (including our overuse of the word "pivot"). One of the common refrains we heard across our conversations was a general lament about people not being able to gather in the kitchen. Pre-pandemic, for many people the kitchen was the heart of their home, the place where people lingered while one led the cooking and the rest gave an assist when called upon. True, there was usually a pecking order, one voice guiding all the others, but the common goal and the camaraderie overshadowed any sense of hierarchy. Many grieved the loss of that communal space.

"Community" has become something of a buzzword in our culture. In an age when people feel more isolated and alone, everyone from politicians to advertisers is attempting to tap into our desire to belong. We tend to associate that belonging with institutions that have deep roots and branches that reach out infinitely. Our faith communities reach back centuries to find their roots. Our communities of color gather, with shared backgrounds, cultures, foods, and goals. Some of us work hard to trace our families back to countries of origin. We find identity in institutions that were there long before we came along and will be there long after we are gone. And we often build community around those steadfast identities.

The community that happens in the kitchen is . . . different. In the kitchen, we form communities that are snapshots in time. They are precious because they are fleeting. It is also often private, happening in our own homes, with only those we've invited in present. It's a brief moment of shared space, common purpose, and like-mindness. Yet from this ephemeral community, we can learn a great deal about the kinds of communities we want to see in the world and to which we want to belong.

Cooking together takes much of the chore out of trying to create community. Communal cooking is often filled with conversation, storytelling, and laughter.

Even in those moments when it is silent, it is often the kind of silence that comes from people who appreciate each other's company and don't need words to show that appreciation. People who cook together often get to know each other's tastes, timing, and tendencies. The interaction of two or more people who are used to being with each other in the kitchen resembles a well-choreographed dance or a well-oiled machine.

Cooking together for the first time, on the other hand, often looks a bit more like *The Muppet Show*. It's chaotic, clumsy, awkward, and hilarious. These things, too, have great value, as a big part of being in community is learning to be vulnerable with one another. Strong relationships are often about dealing with people's metaphorical messes and moving forward through them, while the kitchen gives the added benefit of teaching us to deal with each other's literal messes. A strong community can compensate for its members' weaknesses and accentuate its members' strengths without losing the sense that every member is valuable.

In our podcast, we had an intergenerational interview with the McOsker family, who talked about how cooking is a communal act in their family. Families cooking together can epitomize a communal kitchen. For instance, Nella McOsker, the youngest member of the family we interviewed, reflected on the idea of the kitchen as a family gathering space. "Whenever there's a family event, you find yourself packed in the kitchen. . . . I can picture the family sharing memories and doing the cooking together." Nella noted the way family dynamics played out in the kitchen. While there was a dedicated time to learn recipes with her grandmother, her kitchen had a clear pecking order. "It was very clear that that was not our realm, and you didn't get in there and mess with the flow or do anything other than the specific task that she gave you." Her mother's kitchen, by contrast, was one where anyone could be called upon to do anything. "If you were walking by, you were getting roped into something because something was probably burning."

Nella told us that learning the recipes was wonderful, but that hearing the stories from her Nonna moved her the most. "Hearing Nonna describe her childhood," she said, "these scenes from Italy. It gave me a greater appreciation of just how much we have now. Just as a result of time—electricity, appliances, and all those conveniences that make it so much easier to cook now."

In recent years, the now young-adult grandkids have begun to set up times for everyone to cook together with Nonna and learn all her recipes. They have gathered around in her kitchen to make pasta from scratch, and to learn how to make her signature tomato sauce. At Christmas time they make Cavachinit and Chirrchiskiad cookies. This time and space of intergenerational cooking is marked by storytelling and laughter.

Cooking together is a great way to learn things about our own family history. It's also an invitation to learn more about other people's cultures through the stories behind their foods and eating practices. The kitchen can become a place of cultural exchange when we make space for new recipes and ingredients, but we learn even more when we get the chance to cook alongside someone whose culinary experience might differ wildly from our own.

Narshita Bhargava offered us a story about bringing her Indian culture into a new living situation and a new kitchen. "Before I [moved to the United States], my parents were like, 'You know your food stinks and it's not super accepted in the US. So you really have to navigate your way around, because most Indians who go to the US tend to live with other Indian people.'" She described trying to alter her schedule so that her food didn't offend her housemates. "I tried to figure out all three of their schedules and when no one [would be] home, so that I could cook for the whole day." Ultimately, a conversation with her roommate Nora made her change her approach. "She told me that if someone had a problem, then it was on them because I had to eat. It was important for someone to come and tell me that because it would have taken months on my own." The result was that their kitchen became a place where they learned more about each other's cultures over chai, and shared in each other's cultural celebrations. And it turned out that her roommates loved it when she cooked Indian food!

THE KITCHEN AS A PLACE FOR EVERYONE

Nikki Cooley shared how, when she was growing up on the reservation, cooking happened both indoors and outdoors, and was often a fully intergenerational family event. "When I was a young girl under the Navajo Nation, in my small family homestead we often cooked outside in a place called *cha cha*, which is kind of like a shack house, made out of wood and tree branches for shade. It was kind of like Indian cooking on open fires, using a lot of cast-iron pots and pans. You put a metal or an iron grill over the hot coals, and then you put down maybe mutton or cow or even just vegetables searing on there. We also made that dry bread. It is kind of similar to tortillas, but thicker. We'd make our own dough and put it on there, and that smell when the hot coal kind of singes it—that smell comes. It transports me back to growing up and cooking alongside my family."

For Nikki, cooking alongside her family often meant cooking with her grandmothers. "I was so fortunate to be around a lot of matriarchs talking a mile a minute and also giving out orders. The sound of the slap of the bread between their hands as they flattened it while they stood around talking or maybe gossiping"— those moments are her favorite memories. While they had modern kitchens, in summer heat or even on just warmer days, it made more sense to cook outside where it was cooler. And the cleanup was easier, and they had easy access to wood to feed the fires and whatever else they needed. "Even now, in a modern kitchen when I get those smells, I am transported back to my childhood. And some of us still cook that way."

Nikki points us to a powerful goal of a just kitchen: that the space is *everyone*'s space, that it is a place in the house where everyone has a role and a spot and a way to contribute. Nikki noted that in many other communities or households, the kitchen or cooking area is thought of as women's space, "but in our family or community, it's known as everyone's space. There's lots of laughter, lots of teasing, and it's just so much fun."

She described the kitchen as a matrix, with space for everyone, even if it was and still is clear which bosses ran the show. "They're the ones that have the final say, and you look to them for direction or guidance—including how to properly make dough. How to properly cut up meat or vegetables. The right time to add these ingredients. What time should you be starting them the night before or early in the morning. Before butchering a sheep, providing prayer, providing thanks. The men are talking too—I just happen to hear my matriarch's voices over everybody else's.

And there is space for learning and making mistakes too. "There is always a little bit of a sharp tongue, 'Don't mess around with that. Don't do this, don't do that!' But mistakes are allowed to happen. That's one thing I learned, that we can always know that mistakes will happen, but they can't keep happening. And there's always two aunties or a grandma who is yelling out directions from across the room. And it's just beautiful. It's just so much fun. Kids are running in and out—being careful of sharp objects, the hot spaces, and whatnot—but kids are allowed to be in that space. And they might be asked to do something to help out. We don't keep anyone out, but no one can get away with it if we know someone's missing and not pulling their weight."

BEING A COMMUNITY OF ONE

While we both have families now, the memories of cooking for one aren't too far behind us, and we know that for some, being a community of one is a purposeful choice that brings joy and contentment. But during the times when we were single, it was hard to overlook a glaring fact: many things in our society are geared toward families. Unless we are living alone ourselves, it is easy to miss how obvious that is. For those who live alone, this can be alienating within communities. Unfortunately, the kitchen often becomes yet another place where people living solo are given the message that they are alone, that something is incomplete. This can be especially true in faith communities, but Holly Stallcup, the director of Rise, an organization dedicated to seeing women thrive in church settings, has a different take. She talks about how faith communities often adopt the values of suburban culture, including putting emphasis on families to the exclusion of different life choices for people living solo. She believes that the church often has a "small, thin definition of 'family'" that is harmful to faith communities and doesn't account for the many ways people live life and make choices. Even packaging in our stores says "family" or "multiples," often forcing those who live alone to purchase more than they need, wasting food. Food is often packaged in serving sizes that assume multiple people are eating it. A package of sprouts or even a half gallon of milk can go bad before it's used, when only one person is consuming it. "Those of us trying to be ethical consumers and concerned about the environment—where does that leave us?" Holly asked. This quandary led her back to farmers' markets, which actually do a good job of making things accessible for people purchasing for any number of eaters. A solo purchaser can easily buy a single tomato for a week of sandwiches and a few carrots rather than a jumbo bag.

For people living alone, connecting with those in larger households can often be mutually beneficial. Holly mentioned that it can be a good idea for those living with a partner or as part of a larger community to share a meal invitation—or even a food-shopping outing—with others who might appreciate being added to their number. "It's just looking at the people that you're already in relationship with. Just saying 'Hey, I'm going to double this recipe and bring you half,'" or inviting them to be part of that meal. It's also reciprocal. When neighbors and friends and family are exhausted, sometimes a neighbor running an errand or offering food prep or saying they'd love to make a meal and share it is a way communities of one can turn into larger communities, as they share tasks. As Holly says, "Why don't we share that burden, and then we all eat better and are also better stewards of our money?" Sometimes, too, large memberships to co-ops or bulk-purchase stores might not make economic sense for a family of one, but sharing a membership with others helps keep everyone included in the community with access to affordable food.

Communities of one have their own flexibility, where the generations can be invited in through recipes, and cooking on your own can offer a deeply reflective time of spiritual contemplation or artistic expression. While for some, cooking alone is, well, lonely, for others, it's a way to connect to different food cultures, local communities, and local food vendors in unique and flexible ways. To test foods that don't need to meet the needs of everyone at the table—just one. To savor the quiet winding down of a day. To engage in a healing journey with time for reflection that might open new discoveries. Communities of one might also gather for vivid times of sharing: a Friday meal at one person's home, and exchange meals on Tuesday and Sunday at others'. There are so many ways to be self-companioning and to also, when it seems good to do so, enter into circles of friendship and wider community.

Ultimately, cooking for oneself is an act of self-love in which we should all partake on occasion. In the same way that we say "I love you" to our families and communities through food, we have the responsibility to say the same to ourselves. We have to occasionally remind ourselves that we, too, are worthy of a lovingly prepared meal and that the ability to receive love from others begins with receiving it from ourselves. It's not selfish to love ourselves in that way. It's a reminder that our seeking a better world must include seeking what is good for us as well.

Cooking Together
Derrick's Story

My wife and I have been adopted by the Ruthers, a family from the church she used to serve. A few years back, they invited us to be part of a cooking class with them. Shannon and I joined JoAnn, her two adult children, and her son's fiancée in a brownstone in downtown Baltimore that has been converted into a studio for people to learn to cook. We learned how to make pasta, a task that is just easy enough and just delicate enough to bring out everyone's playful, competitive side. We laughed about uneven noodles and my uncanny ability to get flour everywhere. At the end, we shared a nice meal and patted ourselves on the back for being such accomplished culinary artists.

The Ruthers also facilitated another cooking class experience for Shannon and me. The chef prepackaged all the ingredients we would need to make the recipe during the class. We picked them up and that evening joined maybe two dozen others over Zoom. While the instructor kept his camera on the food during its preparation, we could see the other class participants who left their cameras on. It was clear that there were varying degrees of comfort in the kitchen around the screen. Shannon and I maintained our playful teasing of each other. The overall atmosphere of the class was supportive as we cheered each other's preparation and applauded each other's results. For Shannon and me, it ended up being a lovely night. We laughed as we maneuvered around each other in our small kitchen, took frequent wine breaks, and enjoyed a delicious meal we would never have thought up on our own.

I find that cooking together—on Zoom or off—with different people we invite into our lives, even if only for the time of a shared class, creates an atmosphere of safe vulnerability, which is a vital component of any healthy community. People want to have a space where they can make mistakes and know they will still be accepted. We need spaces where we don't take ourselves so seriously. Whether we are cooking with friends, family, or strangers, the kitchen can provide a space that is conducive to building community and strengthening relationships.

Open Table Night
Anna's Story

Establishing community in new places can be difficult, something my husband and I discovered in the year after we got married and moved. Inspired by authors Leslie Verner and Courtney Ellis to have a weekly night when we routinely opened our kitchen table up for guests, we decided to come up with a plan. I loved the idea of having people over, but often got stuck with the dual barriers of schedules and preparing for guests. Taking Leslie's advice, we picked one night a week to host, followed by Courtney's advice of having a few simple meals we could put together quickly with ingredients we had on hand. Committing to these two practices together helped us to get over the inertia of never remembering to put it on the calendar and the self-imposed pressure to cook a fancy dinner if we invited folks over.

After choosing a night we could commit to each week, we empowered each other to invite one to three people a week. We quickly found joy not only in having people over, who we then got to know better, but also in seeing people reconnect and get to know one another better. As we watched our disparate communities come together, we deepened our own sense of connection and saw new connections forged. Some weeks there was only a person or two, others we had to spill out into the living room, but every time we found community being built.

JUST INVITE PEOPLE OVER

A number of people we've spoken to on our podcast have talked about loneliness and the struggles over making community and finding belonging in the world. One of the huge sacrifices we all had to make during the pandemic was forgoing hospitality. Losing the ability to have people into our homes, make them feel welcomed, and offer them a good meal was devastating for many for whom that was how they liked to build community.

Yet, even before the pandemic, people experienced this reality. Whether it's the phenomenon of frequent moving, the continued polarization of our country, or any other reason holding us back from being in community, many of us can relate to this feeling of loss. Leslie Verner, in her book *Invited: The Power of Hospitality in an Age of Loneliness*, talks about her own journey of loneliness and how someone took the time to break through and invite her into community.

Within Leslie's first three years in a town she had just moved to, she visited eighteen churches or more, seeking a faith community. She told a story about attending one church service for the first time, where no one spoke to her. Even the communion meal "was kind of off in the corner, so you couldn't make a connection with a human being. You had to wander over by yourself and take communion."

She reflected, "It was very lonely, just showing up to churches, not knowing people and not feeling connected." Through that time, when she and her partner reached out and invited others over, it was never reciprocated. "It wasn't until about three years ago, when I was writing my book, that I asked myself, *Who actually did invite us over?* I asked my son, 'Can you think of anybody that has invited us over?' Interestingly, his reply was that our Iranian friends had, and he started listing off people who were all from other countries. And I realized that we'd been invited over more often by our international friends than we had by other Americans we've met."

Leslie reminisced about the simplicity of these invitations and offerings: Sometimes there weren't enough chairs for all. (Why would an international student buy a bunch of furniture if they were only here for a few years?) They would drink juice out of mugs, and the kids would have meals on the floor—with great joy! "It was more about the relationships," Leslie realized, than about fulfilling precise "shoulds" around hosting.

"I don't want to shame anyone, because there are plenty of times when I just don't have the energy to invite people over," she said. "If I'm not intentional about even keeping a list of people I want to invite over or reserving a night a week or a night a month to have guests, it doesn't happen. We are such a planning society, and I think we plan to try to avoid what could maybe be an uncomfortable time."

But Leslie reminded us that the anxiety is often only in the pre-arrival time. "I've also noticed that I only feel uncomfortable until somebody walks in our door. Once people are here, I enjoy them so much. And once they leave, I'm so glad that happened. I think if we can just get over that initial hump of knowing we are going to feel uncomfortable, we are going to feel anxious, we are going to feel nervous, and that our guests also might feel awkward, [it will be okay]." The intentionality to do it anyway helps us move through the speed bumps on the road to community in the kitchen.

Leslie spoke about how reading the gospel stories of Jesus challenged her to open up her home in different ways. She pored over all the stories where Jesus welcomes strangers and eats with tax collectors (seen as the political gougers of the day). "I felt like Jesus was always looking for people on the fringes. And as I examined my own life, . . . when I got out to my perimeters, to the people that are actually on the fringes of my life, I realized, *I don't have the capacity left for people in those spaces where Jesus hung out.*" She went on to speak about what she learned: "that through different seasons and stages of life, our circles can become wider or narrower; there's so much freedom in that."

One gospel story that affected Leslie deeply was one Jesus told, about the good Samaritan on Jericho Road who encounters a Jewish man on the roadside. Two different people from different communities that were often at odds. Yet, the latter was in great need, having been stripped and beaten and left to die. And the Samaritan stops to help him. Leslie found herself struck by how the Samaritan was on the road he was *planning on walking on* when he encountered this person who needed help. "He didn't have to go over, veer over, to all these other roads to see somebody [who needed help]," she mused. "Sometimes I feel I should be visiting the jail, or I should be teaching ESL class—all these things that I want to do to change the world. But right now my kids are two, four, and six years old. I'm limited to where I can go with these small people." And yet, one day, while on a run, she says, "I felt like God said, 'Stay on your Jericho Road, Leslie. Just pay attention. Who is already here?'"

Holding this question in her heart, Leslie was getting ready to take her kids to the river one day, when a twelve-year-old girl from the neighborhood walked over to their yard. "I felt like I should invite her. And then I thought, *But that's more complicated. It's just me taking care of all the kids.* I had this internal wrestling." But ultimately, she did invite the girl, checking in with a guardian to okay it, and thought, *She's on my Jericho Road.* The girl told them her family didn't go out much. "So she came with us, and it was wonderful. . . . She was digging in the dirt with my kids."

Leslie pointed out that this girl was literally on the road where Leslie lives. "This is not a conceptual thing. Who is actually on your literal road in life?" She said she had never wished she *hadn't* invited someone over—that's never a regret. The regret is usually wishing we had—even though it might have been harder. "[But] it wasn't even harder," she laughed. "It was just my own . . . whatever," she said, about her hesitation.

"There is something to be said for getting out of your own comfort zone," Leslie noted. "But often it doesn't take that much. You don't have to go too far to find someone God wants you to invite into your life."

This is the work of hospitality. It is knowing it might be a little uncomfortable, or a little more work, or more about overcoming our own mental blocks. But we can do it anyway. It can be easy for us to talk about loving neighbors or being dedicated to our community, but actually inviting in our new immigrant neighbors or a struggling family we meet in the course of a day—people in need? Or inviting the person living next door with those yappy dogs? Or the neighbor who parks their car where you wish they wouldn't? If we can't do it on our own blocks, are we really going to do it "for the sake of a better world" in a more regional, global context?

THE KITCHEN AS THE KINGDOM OF LOVE AND JUSTICE

Jesus's ministry happened in the context of the Roman Empire, at a time when the caesars declared themselves "sons of God." The kingdom of Rome was the present reality. Over against that reality, Jesus proclaimed that there was a different way to live in the world, a different set of standards: a kingdom of God built on love, justice, and peace in direct opposition to a kingdom built on violence, oppression, and extraction. Our hope is that our kitchens can look more like the kingdom of God than like the empire of Rome.

The author Rachel Held Evans famously wrote: "This is what God's kingdom is like: a bunch of outcasts and oddballs gathered at a table, not because they are rich or worthy or good, but because they are hungry, because they said yes. And there's always room for more." Substitute *kitchen* for "table" and her quote continues to hold true. Our kitchens can become places where people show up and are given a job and made to feel part of the family. Our kitchens can become refuges for those seeking a safe family feel or seeking to be pulled out of self-isolation. Our kitchens can be that place where love and justice are our reality, our way of living justly in the world: people gathered around the stove and the cutting boards, hands busy, hearts open, not because they are rich or worthy or good, but because we and they are hungry. Because together we said yes, and because there is always room for more.

The Rev. Dr. Martin Luther King Jr. offered us a version of this community of justice. He called it "the beloved community." King felt that the beloved community was attainable here and now; it was, in fact, the end goal he was striving for in all of his work. At the end of the day, King didn't see the movement that he was creating as a means of gaining political power, but instead, he was striving for a "truly brotherly society, the creation of the beloved community." How can we imagine our kitchens as places where, even briefly, that kind of community is created?

WHAT GIVES YOU HOPE?
Nikki Cooley

What gives me hope? This is one of my favorite questions. I think about my matriarchs and how they went through what they went through. I wouldn't be here—living the best life and thriving in the way that I can—without them. It started from time immemorial—the long walk through life, including my grandmother's struggle with breast cancer and other hardships, getting married, raising children on their own, praying and making offerings to the holy ones, going through ceremony . . . so I could be here.

My daughter was born twelve years ago. The labor was one of the hardest things I've ever done. It was painful. But my husband, my partner in life, said to me, "Remember what your matriarchs went through so you could be here, giving birth to our first daughter. Remember, your grandmother said she gave birth to your father beside a juniper tree by herself at night?" That gives me hope. Imagine feeling alone and in pain, and yet you're bringing a beautiful life into the world. And then he grew up to be an amazing man who gave her amazing grandchildren.

So my ancestors survived, which means I can be here, and that really does give me hope—as do my children. I have two of the happiest children, and they just give me so much hope every day. It's hard to stay grumpy around them. It's the matriarchs, my ancestors, and my children that give me great hope.

Lentil Soup and No-Knead Bread

Alissa Wilkinson

For me, a big pot of soup and a loaf of bread is the ideal large-group, low-budget meal. When I was in my mid-twenties, living in a 500-square-foot studio apartment with my husband, the 2008 recession hit. We were both still employed—me steadily in tech writing, him intermittently in film production—but many of our artist friends were struggling, and in an effort to do something, I hit upon the idea of hosting a monthly brunch in our tiny home to which all of our friends and their friends were invited. You didn't have to RSVP, and you didn't have to bring anything, though both were welcome.

This went on for a couple of years, during which we might have upward of twenty-five people pile into our small place. Everyone sat on the floor, and because there wasn't really anywhere to put a plate down, bowl-friendly food was ideal. I also never knew if the attendees would be vegetarian or dairy-free or have some other dietary restriction, and we couldn't afford to buy enormous quantities of more expensive foods, so I figured out that lentils can stretch a very long way.

Recipes

The Soup

INGREDIENTS

1 sizable onion, or some shallots, peeled and chopped relatively small

2–4 cloves garlic (you can never have too much garlic)

1–2 ribs celery, chopped small

1–2 carrots, chopped small (just scrub, no need to peel)

1 cup lentils (green or French ones, probably; save the red ones, which get mushy and thick, for other splendid uses)
1 quart water or any kind of broth, if you have it (I confess: I use bouillon a lot, as my freezer is too small to keep homemade broth around)
A glug of extra-virgin olive oil
Salt and pepper
A bay leaf, if you have one

DIRECTIONS

1. Dump some oil into a pot—I use a ceramic-coated dutch oven—and heat it to medium-high. When the oil looks like it's glistening a little, add the onion and cook down, stirring often, till it's tender and becoming translucent; this usually takes about 5–6 minutes, but it can vary depending on your stovetop.

2. When the onions are almost ready, add the garlic and cook for another minute, stirring. Add carrots and celery. Salt and pepper them well, and cook for a few more minutes.

3. Then pour in the lentils, water or broth, and a bay leaf. Bring it to a boil, then let it simmer for about 30–40 minutes, till the lentils are at a texture you like. Ladle into bowls and serve with a swirl of olive oil on top.

So here are some things you can add to lentil soup: chunks of potato; a little cumin; some thyme or any chopped fresh herb you can think of (with the possible exception of mint, though that might even work); cayenne pepper, dried red pepper flakes, or paprika for a bit of kick; green beans; chopped tomatoes from a can or tomato paste; kale or spinach, roughly chopped; a swirl of yogurt or croutons or both on top. Or anything else that seems good to you. If you mess it up, you'll just be learning a valuable lesson for next time, and honestly, you're probably the only person who will notice.

The Bread

A few years ago I discovered no-knead artisanal bread and I've never looked back. The traditional way of making bread requires a considerable head start, and I can't seem to plan for meals that far ahead. So I was delighted to discover there's a quicker way to make it.

I love this bread because it has four ingredients, if you don't count water. I've adapted this recipe from Mark Bittman, who knows a thing or two about simple home-cooked food.

INGREDIENTS

3 cup flour (they will tell you bread flour, and if you've got it, great, but you can get away with other kinds of flour too)

1 packet instant yeast, which comes out to 2 teaspoons if you don't use the packets
1 1/2 teaspoons salt
Some olive oil

DIRECTIONS

1. Put the flour, yeast, and salt in a big bowl with lots of extra space. Add 1 1/2 cups warmish water and stir it all around. If you're accustomed to making bread, it will look completely wrong right now—all shaggy and floury. Do not fear! Help is on the way.
2. Cover the bowl with plastic wrap or something tight-fitting and leave it alone for four hours or so in a warm place. It will rise to about double in size.
3. Smear oil onto your counter and turn the dough out onto it. (I usually make sure my hands are coated in oil to help this along.) You are not going to knead it! You simply need to fold it over on itself twice, then take the plastic wrap and cover it right there on the counter. Let it sit for 30 minutes.
4. While it's sitting, preheat your oven to 450 degrees, and put the vessel in which you intend to bake the bread into the oven so it can heat up too.

I tend to use a deep cast-iron pan with a lid, or a dutch oven. You can use Pyrex or a casserole dish or whatever you have, as long as it's deep and has a lid.

5. When the dough is finished rising, pull the pan out of the oven and put it on the stovetop for a moment. Carefully pick up the dough with your hands and flip it into the pan, seam side up. It will sizzle just a little as the dough makes contact with the hot pan. With a potholder, grab the pan, and shake it once or twice to get the dough well-distributed.

6. Put the top on the pan and return it to the oven for 30 minutes. Then take the lid off and let it bake for an additional 15–30 minutes. (I usually err on the lower side, as I like to be able to bite through the bread with ease, but crust enthusiasts may feel differently.) The crust will look beautifully browned. When you take it out, slide a fork or a spatula underneath the loaf to loosen it and turn it out onto a cooling rack. If you don't have a cooling rack—like me, a person who has never managed to remember to buy a cooling rack in her life—you can put it on a plate and it should be fine.

7. When it's cooled off a little, slice it up and serve it with room-temperature butter or cheese, and a bowl of delicious lentil soup.

LITURGY
God's Kitchen

We're welcome in God's kitchen,
Just because
We belong to God
And we belong to one another.

We're welcome in God's kitchen,
On good days and bad,
When we're grieving,
When we're celebrating,
When we're craving community,
And when we want to be alone.

We're welcome in God's kitchen,
To create and to be fed,
To connect and celebrate,
To heal and to be nurtured,
And to be transformed
Into God's Beloved Community Kitchen.

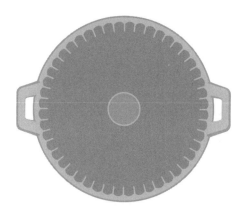

CHAPTER 8

THE KITCHEN AS A PLACE OF MUTUALITY

Sharing food together is one of the first things we often think of when the word "hospitality" comes up. Be it cheese and crackers before an event, soup and salad with friends around your table, or a local food program, food is a way we show our care and welcome to other people. Yet that care and welcome can quickly turn into a misuse of power as we get caught in roles of "haves and have-nots," where ownership of food and discrepancies around who is "worthy" to receive it turn acts of collective eating into transactions rather than mutual sharing.

In this chapter, we'll explore what a just kitchen looks like when it is feeding groups of people—be it participation in a community kitchen, or a church kitchen or our home kitchens opened up to the community in various ways. We'll look at supporting systems of food sovereignty in communities, as opposed to toxic food charity. As we explore examples of groups cooking for people experiencing food insecurity, we'll keep a particular eye on ways mutuality, respect, and care for the dignity of all are engaged in shared kitchens.

As we've written earlier, kitchens have long been spaces of unequal power dynamics. Historically, that inequality has had racial, gender, and class components, creating separations between those who serve and those who are served. But hospitality, when practiced with mutual respect, is one way the just kitchen disrupts inequality—because the one serving does so not out of obligation but out of love and a desire to show guests care.

Ironically, one of the times hospitality sometimes gives way to unhealthy power dynamics is when well-meaning people attempt to be of service. For those on the receiving end of food offered in charity, there's a cost: it may be a loss of choice as well as a loss of personal dignity. Organizations with the intention of helping often make hurtful decisions about who is and who is not worthy of being served. Those served often endure judgment about their character and lifestyle. Religious organizations are particularly prone to this and often have strings attached to their hospitality, requiring a confession of faith or that participants listen to a sermon before they are fed.

We believe that *any* kitchen can be one where people are served with dignity and respect. There are feeding programs that treat those who enter their doors as honored guests. There are places where people can come in off the street and enjoy a good meal without judgment or conditions. A just kitchen is one in which mutual relationships exist between those who are cooking and those who are invited to the table. And while the previous chapter was about cooking *in* community, here we explore what it looks like to cook *for the sake of* community.

Our colleague Hugh Hollowell used to live in North Carolina, working with people experiencing homelessness. He makes a direct connection between food and relationships—so much so that he titled his most recent book *Food Is Love*. Hugh is a natural storyteller, and one particular story he's told, now lovingly referred to as "Biscuitgate," has gotten a lot of attention.

As he tells it, shortly after he moved to North Carolina and started working with people living on the streets, Hugh began to notice that many of the feeding programs in the community had a religious component, forcing people to listen to a sermon before they could be fed. And, he pointed out, "these were not wonderful sermons. These were 'You're gonna burn in hell forever' sermons. And you already feel like you're in hell, because you're there and hungry." The disrespect for guests offended Hugh to his core, and the only place he could find a solution was his own kitchen.

So the Saturday after this realization, he cooked twenty-four sausage biscuits and took them to the park where people often gathered. They said, "When does the preaching start?" Hugh responded, "I don't know anything about preaching. I've just got some food." Hugh's philosophy was simple: when asking, *Do people need food?*, if the answer is yes, then make food for people. No strings attached. "When you share food with no expectations, you are encountering God."

Unsurprisingly, a community formed around Hugh's simple act. Others, including churches, began feeding people simply because they needed food. And what formed were new relationships. "The other thing I love about sharing food with people," said Hugh, "is that it opens us up to unlikely relationships. People at our table tend to be just like us, but that day in the park, there were people experiencing houselessness, there were people wandering by, there was a police officer who stopped to talk. It opened up room for unlikely relationships." There's no denying that a power dynamic still exists in this situation, and often that dynamic is inescapable when we are trying to be of service, but being mindful of what we ask from those we hope to serve is a step toward leveling the playing field. Are we trying to manipulate or ask for an unearned vulnerability, or are we serving simply because the person across from us is a human being deserving of love and care? These are the questions that well-intentioned people in positions to offer service must contend with.

Another colleague who understands how food facilitates relationships is Justin Cox, who we've mentioned previously. Justin calls himself a "Black Sheep Baptist" in his online interactions. He's also a pastor. Justin moved to Vermont to take on leadership of a new church shortly before the pandemic began. Unable to gather in the usual ways, Justin found a way to connect with the members of his small New England village. He would wake every morning and begin to cook with a specific member of the community in mind. "I could just see them through the door, visit from a distance, and hand them a bag of food. That became the way for me to live out that call." This soon extended beyond the church to the people in his community, becoming a way for the village to know his face and for him to be present for them. As truly hospitable food-sharing often does, Justin's outreach engendered mutual exchange. People began to say, "We appreciate this, but can we give you something too?" There's a mantra in his community that you don't return an empty container. In both giving and receiving, Justin engaged the community. As he spoke with his neighbors, he learned why certain foods and recipes were important to them, and he got to hear family stories and gain insights into the lives around him. These exchanges of meals and treats and histories served as a form of communication. "It's an ongoing, never-ending conversation," he said, which he and others found profoundly meaningful.

Feed and Be Fed
Anna's Story

The ability for everyone to contribute is a value we see time and time again when it comes to group cooking. Yes, humans share the need to be physically fed, but also many share the need to be able to offer to other people and contribute to the fabric of society. So often when people are struggling and have physical needs that are unmet, toxic givers focus on what they can provide for them, failing to mutually engage and find common invitation for all to care for each other.

At the Garden Church, the urban farm and outdoor sanctuary I planted in Los Angeles in 2014, we did a lot of things together. We worked in the garden, planting and weeding and watering and harvesting. We gathered and turned the compost and built new trellises and tied up tomato plants. Sunday gatherings were held in that same space, with the ground beneath our feet and the sky as our roof. And then we ate together. A beautiful swath of humanity gathered around the community meal: some for whom that was their only meal of the day, others who would have otherwise been eating alone in their apartment, and others who found that community gathering was a different kind of nourishment. It was a time of connection and community for all of us.

We ate together around picnic tables in a city lot and learned together about growing food that was then cooked and enjoyed. The Garden Church community meal uniquely involved the full circle from growing the food, to eating the food, to composting the leftovers. Even as the cooking element was primarily done in people's home kitchens, on Fridays community members often came to

(continued)

harvest whatever was in season and then take it home to cook for the Sunday community meal.

On any given Sunday, you'd find an eighty-seven-year-old grandmother and former nun bringing in large vats of polenta, with Swiss chard from the garden laced through it. A fifth-grade boy and two of his friends might come in with a huge batch of pesto pasta made with an abundance of basil. One woman, who proclaimed herself lonely and didn't want to eat alone, brought in a vegetable medley made with the harvest. All of these people circled around, and we'd ask each other, "What's on our table today? Tell us about where the food came from." As people shared about the dishes they'd brought, others cheered and expressed appreciation in anticipation for the food they were about to eat. While eating, recipes were shared and connections made.

"I never knew how to cook mustard greens," one person said to another.

"It makes me so happy to see the food I cooked being enjoyed," said someone else.

"It's rather poignant to think that I was part of planting those seeds and tending the crops that we're now eating," another reflected.

While the kitchen was not right there, bustling with people cooking together, the act of cooking with food that had been communally grown and then sharing that food together in community completed a circle. A circle in which we were all held.

While most of the time the food was made in people's personal kitchens, a few makeshift kitchen moments happened right there in the garden or at the picnic tables—often salads were prepared there. Being in California, there was rarely a time of year without something that could be harvested for a salad—be it tender lettuce greens in the cooler season, or tomatoes and basil in the heat. Anyone who showed up could be part of creating this culinary offering, starting with harvesting into a wicker basket, and then moving to the outdoor sink and the salad spinner that lived there expressly for this purpose. Often fresh herbs and even edible flowers bedecked these green offerings, and people who didn't have kitchens to cook in found great joy in being able to create a kitchen right there and contribute.

The motto of the Garden Church is "Feed and be fed," with the goal of feeding body, mind, and spirit. It is embedded at the center of the Garden Church community that this is a mutual effort.

EVERYONE HAS SOMETHING TO OFFER

When people work side by side, each contributes something to the work. The same is true in the kitchen. Give your guest the job of peeling the potatoes, and they become part of the family. Invite the college student who lives across the street to bring their friends; expect everyone to pitch in and do the dishes, and they'll know that they belong.

It is heartening to see more and more examples of organizations and groups paying attention not just to the physical needs of people who are hungry but also to the human needs for dignity and choice, mutuality and contribution. For instance, at the Manna Community Kitchen, the dignity and care of those coming to eat are at the forefront of the organization's values.

Lee Anderson, one of the head cooks and a stalwart leader in the community, talks about the importance of meeting people where they are, calling the Manna Community Kitchen a "zero-judgment zone." Lee looks for ways to eliminate rules that don't *need* to be there, rules that could get in the way of connection: "We used to have a rule that you couldn't come in more than half an hour before the meal start time. I was like, 'Well, what is the point of that? Somebody is waiting out in the parking lot in the rain?' If we're here and you're here, come into the room. Share with us. Get comfortable with us." In the spirit of "Do no harm" and trauma-informed service, the community kitchen is committed to people eating together in a space that offers dignity and care.

"If five people come to that door, we'll meet [them each] differently," Lee said. "We sit and eat with the guests and hear their stories. And some of them are amazing."

In a newly refinished dining space, one of the guests said to him one night, "I can't believe we get to eat in a room with art."

"That sentence just broke my heart," said Lee. "Of course you get to. I hate the fact that you wouldn't assume that this is something you would be invited to." He added, "We're trying to exceed expectations."

Another way Manna Community Kitchen lives out its values of mutuality and dignity is that everyone sits down and eats together. The priest of the hosting church (St. John's Episcopal in Northampton, Massachusetts), the guests, the volunteers, the person visiting from out of town—they are all invited to come and sit together in one big dining room. Lee talks about how guests who are food-insecure are often surprised to learn that folks who have access to other foods are eating the same food they are. This is not simply an act of solidarity on the part of the privileged in the community; it is also because the food is amazing! Locally sourced as much as possible, lovingly prepared, and absolutely delicious, this food honors the dignity of all people and nourishes them accordingly. In thinking about his own journey, Lee shared, "I didn't start to get healthy in my life until I cared about *me*. . . . Food gives us an easy way to express care."

Lee's story lifts up for us the fact that food as invitation upholds the dignity of people. It lets us know our worth—there is no limit to the ways we deserve to have our needs met. We all have moments when that message is really hard to receive because of how we might be feeling about ourselves. So to have someone outside of your experience put that meal in front of you communicates that you're worth it, you're absolutely worth cooking for, you're worth taking time to cook for, you're worth setting a place for.

Cooking for others was having a major impact on Lee, but does that also translate to his life outside of the community kitchen? Lee reflected that everyone who trusts him to feed them will say hello on the street. "They know that we care for them. They care for those of us who are cooking. They start to care for each other." Lee talked about one kid who would come in but would hardly ever eat. I thought, *Why are you not eating? My food is okay*. So I asked him, and he said, 'Well, I'm diabetic, so I can't have this.' The young man had been coming in for weeks, so I said, 'Tell me what you can eat and I will cook it for you!'"

Lee described a photograph he once took, looking from the kitchen through the doorway into the dining room. The picture is of two men, leaning back, chatting.

The meal was long over, everything was cleaned up, and everyone else was gone. One of the men was a volunteer, recently retired as vice president of a major life insurance company. The other was a regular who had come late and thought he'd missed the meal, but Lee had heated something up for him. This was somebody who, the day before, had likely slept alongside a bike path. Both men had very relaxed body language, although they had only met an hour ago, and the comfort struck Lee so deeply that he pulled out his phone and took a picture of two new friends chatting over a meal. "We are just all humans," said Lee. "There isn't a separation."

TOXIC CHARITY

Far too often feeding programs, while well intentioned, can quickly fall into the traps of toxic charity and perpetuating systems of power and privilege. The Rev. Dr. Heber Brown III, founder of the Black Church Food Security network, explains:

> Charity does not equal justice. Charity can mask our understanding of the root of the problem. Prolonged engagement with charity can corrode the soul of those in need; it can wear away our sense of human dignity, our somebody-ness. The flip side is that when economically affluent, often White-led organizations are constantly in the posture of giving, it can also corrode the soul of the giver, who is always in a position of superiority. Food charity is a sweet siren song. It is not a sustainable track toward the Beloved Community.

When we look at just kitchens, it goes well beyond our personal kitchens. The kitchens are in churches and community centers, synagogues and soup kitchens that seek justice. These shared kitchen spaces hold within them understandings of the complex layers of justice and injustice, generosity and power, liberation and oppression—even as just kitchens hold a commonality of dignity and shared food that honors everybody's somebody-ness.

Be Our Guest
Derrick's Story

My wife and I love to have people over. We love to cook for people. We have a dream of opening a retreat center someday. The idea of being able to host people, helping them to rest and rejuvenate, excites us both. For now, we settle for opportunities when we can have people over for dinner or host them in our guest room when they come through town. Both of us would be more than pleased if the thing that we were known for was our hospitality.

*But being hospitable doesn't necessarily come naturally to me. Growing up, ours wasn't the house that friends went to after school or on weekends. We lived in a neighborhood that was quite a bit above our means, so I was self-conscious about not having things that were as nice as what my friends had. I still carry some of that with me today. It's when I host people and also cook for them that some of the self-consciousness goes away. To me, food is an equalizer. A messy house will, in my mind, always be less important than a good meal. What changes when I cook for our guests is that I am not just hosting—I am **serving.***

We've written about the ways that kitchens can reflect harmful power dynamics, with people diminished in the kitchens, cooking for the powerful. But there are times when we willingly subvert that dynamic—like when we cook for a child, a sick partner, or an aging parent. That subversion doesn't shame the person who is unable to do for themselves. It is service, an act of self-sacrifice, that communicates our love for that person. In my spiritual tradition, service is a universal value. Service done well raises others without diminishing ourselves. It reinforces the idea that the person being served is worthy of having good things in their life.

What my wife and I share is a belief that actions speak louder than words—and that, for us, one of the best ways to say "I love you" is through food.

COOKING AS CHURCH

At St. Lydia's, a dinner church in Brooklyn, New York, cooking *is* church, which begins with the chopping of carrots and the sautéing of onions. And the gathering winds down with the washing of dishes and the sweeping of floors. Between these communal acts, you'll find things you might be more familiar with in a church—including a sermon and the sacrament of communion—yet all of these movements are held together as holy.

The Rev. Emily Scott, founder of St. Lydia's, says that everything about the liturgy there is designed to connect people to one another and to create a community of mutuality. She explained that everyone sits around tables, not on pews, so that everyone is facing each other during the gathering. Emily counted something like seventeen different moments of direct engagement during the service, including being greeted by someone who helps you make a name tag, being asked to help set up a table, a candle-lighting where you turn to your neighbor and light your candle from theirs. And sitting at a table means conversation with people, "that sometimes is really wonderful and sometimes is super awkward and weird," she laughed. After the sermon and poem and prayer, you will be asked to wash dishes with people before sharing the peace at the end. "So in a city where, if you live on your own, you could go weeks without human touch, to come to a place where there are so many moments to connect with people on an individual level— that's an example of how the hunger of the community can show up in the liturgy," Emily concluded.

WELCOMING PEOPLE IN THEIR WHOLENESS

There is a story in the Gospels about a shepherd who has one hundred sheep and one of them is lost, so he leaves the other ninety-nine sheep behind to go find the lost one. The story ends with the joy when that one sheep is found and the rejoicing that happens when a person is returned to community.

It's a familiar story to many in the Christian tradition. However, we often miss the frame of the story. Before the parable is told, Jesus is accused by the religious leaders of aligning with and sharing meals with those on the margins. Their criticism of Jesus's inclusive welcome of those deemed undeserving in society brings him to respond with a parable that speaks to the responsibility of those with power: to use their power to seek the lost, to look out for those who are not in the center of religion or culture, to search for people who have been pushed aside. He then points to the joy experienced when the lost one is returned to the community.

In the stories in this chapter, and so many other stories of the kitchen as a place of mutuality, we see this way of Jesus coming to life. When we put ourselves in places of mutual care and connection in shared kitchens, we can see how people are returned to belonging. Each of us is placed in the parable by Jesus when he ends the parable with a question: "Which one of you . . . ?" Jesus calls us to identify with the role of a concerned shepherd and to be a seeker of the lost, always drawing others toward God and into communion/community with one another.

Here's Jesus, eating at the table with those who won't find welcome from mainstream culture. Here's Jesus, living beyond divisions and distrust. Living in ways that overturn the patterns of conquest and power, pointing away from overconsumption and exploitation. Jesus is all about welcoming people in their wholeness—all parts of them, even the parts that are not generally considered acceptable in society.

This goes beyond an easy summary of "Okay, so we should make sure we give welcome and care to our unhoused neighbors or those who are living in poverty." That is right and true. But this gospel calls us to so much more. This gospel calls us to gather around God's table with our whole selves, ready and curious, looking to be in community and find belonging with other whole selves. This gospel calls us to have an awkward conversation with someone we don't know over soup and bread, to learn from the person who walks in the door hungry, and to create kitchens where all kinds of people are honored.

This gospel calls us to seek the way of love on both the micro level and the macro level, to make change in our own beings, and to be part of a global shift. We are called to turn and change so we might be brave enough to show up in God's kitchen as who we are: grumbly, struggling people, often separated from each other. We come into our kitchens with that self, and at the same table— God's table—we eat with others who are also finding the freedom and joy of being changed together.

WHAT GIVES YOU HOPE?
Hugh Hollowell

There is a great story that Virginia Woolf's husband, Leonard, tells in his autobiography *Downhill All the Way*. It was the late 1930s, and Leonard was in his garden, planting iris bulbs, when Hitler came on the radio to make one of his speeches. Virginia Woolf yelled at Leonard to come inside because Hitler was on the radio. And Leonard said, "I shan't do it. I'm planting flowers. And they'll be here long after he's gone."

Everything we do is an opportunity to plant flowers.

I lost my dad to COVID-19 in October 2020. He was a frontline worker. It's not just that we've lost millions of people: each of those people is someone's parent, someone's child, someone's coworker, someone's friend. They are servers at our favorite restaurants. They are the owners of the dry cleaner we go to. Our lives are connected with them in myriad ways.

While we have lost millions of people during this time, there have been babies born, houses bought, children graduating from high school. It probably didn't go the way they thought it would, but still, they've graduated from high school. People are making love. They're planting gardens. They're looking toward the future.

One of my favorite artists said that when you're depressed, you should draw pictures of Batman, because you'll still be depressed, but you will also have a picture of Batman.

So, I'm depressed, but I make biscuits. And now I've got biscuits. Perhaps that's all very woo-woo, but we do have a chance every day to create something new. My friend David Wilmont and I were talking about *saving the world*. And he said, "I think that's naive, but we can definitely *change the world*."

We don't have a choice about that; our very presence disrupts the force. Just the act of being in the world changes the world. So how intentional are we about that change? It does come down to, *Am I going to plant flowers or am I going to listen to Hitler?* And which one moves us closer to that better world that we all dream of and believe to be possible? Sometimes we just need to make biscuits and gravy for dinner. At the end of the day, the opportunity to create a better world than the one we have now, in a thousand different ways, is what gives me hope.

Thai Dressing

Lee Anderson

Manna Community Kitchen loves to use this dressing on top of our Thai beef salad or served with soba noodles (hot or cold). I received this recipe from my late friend Geoff Kiteley, a chef at the former Green Street Cafe in Northampton.

───────── **Recipe** ─────────

INGREDIENTS

1/3 cup rice wine vinegar

1/3 cup salad oil

3 tablespoons soy sauce

1/2 cup peanut butter (add more if it's not thick enough for your liking)

1/4 bunch of lemon grass or cilantro

1 tablespoon crushed red pepper (add more to accommodate your spice level)

Garlic cloves (add as much as you'd like, then double it)

2- or 3-inch piece of ginger, finely chopped

DIRECTIONS

1. Put all ingredients into a blender and blend until smooth.
2. This dressing is great to use right away, but the longer it has to sit, the more the red pepper and ginger influence the rest of the ingredients.

LITURGY
All Are Welcome Here

When we say "all are welcome" we like to think we know what that
means.
But maybe
It's a challenge,
A question
To always be asking.

What is welcome?
To you?
To me?
What does welcome taste like?
How does it feel?
And how do we need to change to make it real?

"All are welcome"
As an invitation,
To lower the counters
And bring out more baking dishes.
To learn new recipes and change our language.
To open ourselves up to the wholeness of other human beings,
And to welcome all of ourselves
As well.

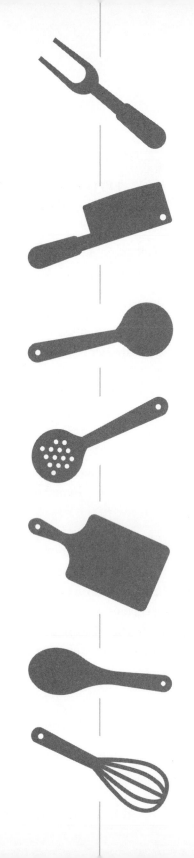

CHAPTER 9

THE KITCHEN AS A PLACE OF CELEBRATION

It's hard to imagine a celebration without food! Be it a birthday cake, an elaborate holiday feast, or a gathering with friends, most celebrations call for food or even have a meal as the focal point. In this chapter, we look at how even our everyday encounters with food can be cause for celebration, and how our larger celebrations can be nurtured from our just kitchens—with no catering or special orders required.

When we pause and reflect in our kitchens, we may find much to celebrate there—from the beauty in the cross-section cut of a tomato, to the delight of the melding flavors of spicy peppers and cool cucumber, to serving a carefully plated colorful dish. Our kitchens become the center of celebrating the most special occasions in our lives, but they can also be a celebration of nature, beauty, and food itself.

HOLY DAY COOKING

Many traditions are a part of holidays—"holy days" that are set apart from the rest of the calendar. They might be national holidays or religious in nature. They may commemorate a change of season, some extraordinary accomplishment, or a somber remembrance. These days break us out of our routines and focus our attention on the world or on others in some particular way.

Celebrations aren't limited to our communal observances, of course. We celebrate birthdays and anniversaries, promotions and new ventures, graduations and retirements. Even funerals are often reframed as celebrations of life. More personal celebrations often feel like they carry more weight than our communal observances. What do these celebrations—corporate, private, and religious—have in common? Food.

Food and drink are central to our enjoyment of life—from birthdays to holidays to tailgates—because they are simply one of life's great joys. Cooking for parties, festivals, and holidays is a completely different endeavor than our everyday activity of making meals. It's often loaded with greater expectation and carries more cultural weight. The foods we make and share in those times are often the backdrops to our most cherished memories.

Celebration is a virtue. It is a value that can be cultivated. Even amid all the hardships and injustices in the world, it is vital that we take time to observe the personal milestones and cultural observances that remind us how rich and full life can be. Celebration isn't simply taking a day away from work, eating ourselves into a food coma, or drinking ourselves into unconsciousness. Celebration is about honoring the goodness of this world. It is a show of gratitude for our communities and the relationships that make life meaningful. Celebration is more than rote practices and stale traditions. A true celebration breathes new life into the ancient and sacred in ways that make them newly alive. And the just kitchen is well situated to meet the task of celebration.

At the same time, we want to recognize the great burden of celebration when we are asked, or expected, to cook for special days. People have certain levels of expectation for how things should be done when marking a special occasion. That heightened expectation can create a higher level of stress combined with fear of disappointing the people we love. That can make celebrations joyous for everyone *except for the one who is in the kitchen*. No one wants to be remembered as the maker of the dry Thanksgiving turkey (see Derrick's story below) or the baker of blueberry pie when everyone was expecting pecan. Cooking for celebrations is its own unique challenge.

In her book *Dare to Lead*, Brené Brown talks about the importance of communicating our expectations. In the context of holidays and cooking, this is a big one. How many of us, steeped in a lifetime of expectations and nostalgia, have said, "We have to have the ____, like ____ always made. That's what makes it my birthday/Christmas/Hanukkah/Thanksgiving." Part of nurturing a just kitchen is to have space for honesty and communication with those connected to us and our kitchens.

Before your next holiday, a new tradition might be to have some conversations about what is important to people in terms of the menu, what feels good in terms of who is doing what cooking and cleaning, and what new ways of celebrating might be welcomed this year. Sometimes switching things up can bring us back to the heart of what we are celebrating in the first place.

Holiday cooking across cultures and religious traditions gives us an opportunity to learn about one another and celebrate together. Housemates Nora and Harshita spoke about their experience of sharing holiday meals. "The four of us in the house came from three different faiths," Nora explained. "We introduced each other to different festivals. In the pandemic, we were each other's bubble—each other's family. I wasn't going to jet off somewhere to celebrate Easter. And Harshita couldn't gather her community outside of our bubble for Diwali. So we celebrated [each holiday] together." They made the whole, traditional meal together, which let them share not only in the celebration, but in the specificity of ingredients, preparation, traditions, and religious background.

Harshita pointed out that it was difficult not having access to many of the traditional ingredients she likes to use. "But I still managed my way around it because I knew I would have someone to celebrate with, someone who was open to celebrating and to whatever I had to offer." That made up for a lot. Her biggest challenge, she said, "was adjusting my heat tolerance. I myself don't have very good heat tolerance, but then we would eat spices in the food! Fortunately, everyone in the house had good tolerance for diverse palates. I cherished all the festivals we celebrated together and felt good about it—like I was a part of something and others were a part of my traditions too."

Nora shared that she often loses the thread between the meal she is eating and the holiday being celebrated. Coming from a Christian tradition, she said, "I have very clear ideas of, for instance, *this* is what you eat on Easter. But there is the celebration at church and afterward there is a meal: I often lose the connection between those events." Harshita said that in India, in most religious households, every meal they make goes to the gods first. "We have a temple inside our house, and you serve the gods the food first," she explained, "and about thirty minutes later, you eat it, because the gods have now blessed your food." Since there are "about three million gods, they're all just sitting there blessing!" This is why, she explained, "we can't taste our food when we're making it—it hasn't been blessed yet. You just wing it and leave it the way it turns out." Even now, out of habit, Harshita still doesn't taste the food while she is in the process of cooking.

FROM FAST TO FEAST

Our relatively inexpensive access to all kinds of food is generally perceived as something positive. The problem with having unfettered access is that our special-occasion foods become less special. In *Soul Food: The Surprising Story of an American Cuisine, One Plate at a Time*, Adrian Miller describes much of what we consider in the genre of "soul food" to be celebration food. Miller reminds us that many of those foods were never meant to be eaten on a daily basis. In recent years, we have seen the health implications of celebration foods becoming everyday foods in many cultures.

Celebratory food might be about breaking the rules—enjoying heightened flavors in abundance—but there comes a point when we break the rules so often that we forget what they are.

We often also forget that traditionally, many of our cultural feast days were balanced by a time of fasting. While significant for Muslim communities with Ramadan, fasting has largely disappeared from other cultures and religious observances. Self-denial is a tough sell. And in some cases, full fasts from food may not be medically or psychologically safe. But fasts can also have a positive impact and play an important role in a just kitchen. In chapter 3 we looked at giving the kitchen itself a sabbath. Fasting can facilitate a time when the kitchen lies dormant in preparation for the feasting that lies ahead.

"Fasting may seem like a cruel test to see if we can deny our bodies food," write Rabbi Irwin Kula and Vanessa L. Ochs in their short essay "Meditation on Fasting." "Yet, at the heart of this practice is a desire to shift our attention away from the body's immediate needs and to focus on spiritual concerns. The logic goes something like this: when we fast, we are faced with admitting our frailty. In that weakened state, we examine the parts of ourselves that are fragile and strengthen them with meditations and supplications."

Fasting can also add to our enjoyment of food once the fast is broken. We can return the "special" to special-occasion foods through periods of denial. And finally, fasting can, for a brief moment, put us in solidarity with those who regularly go hungry. Whether it's creating an experience we've never had before or a reminder of our own lean seasons, fasts can make us mindful of how so many regularly go without.

CELEBRATING CREATION

In his introduction to Wendell Berry's collection *The Art of the Commonplace*, writer-scholar Norman Wirzba refers to food as "the most concrete and intimate connection to the earth that exists." Sourcing our food in ways that support creation and our local communities whenever possible is something we've returned to again and again in this book. But celebrating creation in our kitchen is not only about shopping at farmers' markets. We celebrate creation in our kitchens when we recognize that we are a part of the created order, not standing outside of it or over it. Our kitchens can be places where we show gratitude for nature's abundance and acknowledge our own dependence on the world for our survival.

Shani Mink is the executive director of the Jewish Farmers Network (JFN), a nonprofit organization headquartered in Maryland. Most of the Jewish festivals and holidays were historically rooted in agriculture, she says. The celebrations and their accompanying liturgies remind us that we are dependent on the sun, rain, and soil for everything—from the seed to the harvest. For Shani and the other members of the JFN, work on the farm connects them to their ancient history of celebrating the goodness of the land. "I think the more I put together the pieces of what my ancestors did with crucial pieces of my inherited tradition, as a farmer, [it] helps me experience the Jewish holidays on a much deeper level. I'm part of a thousands-year-old tradition of Jews engaged in land." When she formally celebrates the harvest, for example, she has already been harvesting for months. "I get to celebrate my work. I'm forced to take this break in order to celebrate. I don't think that I had access to this meaning before I was farming."

IS THERE ALCOHOL IN A JUST KITCHEN?

"People use drugs, legal and illegal, because their lives are intolerably painful or dull," writes Wendell Berry in *The Art of the Commonplace*. "They hate their work and find no rest in their leisure. They are estranged from their families and their neighbors. It should tell us something that in healthy societies drug use is celebrative, convivial, and occasional, whereas among us it is lonely, shameful, and addictive. We need drugs, apparently, because we have lost each other." In his signature ability to get to the heart of the matter, Berry brings both understanding and reflection.

This is something we both value, as there are aspects of a just kitchen that hold a lot of complexity and are important to talk about. From the time of this project's inception, we knew that a part of the life of the kitchen is what, for many, accompanies, or is central to, a meal, a barbecue, or a celebration: alcoholic beverages. Some holidays are even defined as "drinking holidays," centered more on drinking than on the actual saint's-day observances. (Looking at you, St. Patty's Day!) And regardless of whether we have given them that specific designation, alcohol is often a big presence at many holiday festivities.

While alcohol seems to be an accepted part of our culture, we also recently observed friends and colleagues choosing to step away from drinking altogether. And with close friends and family members who have been in recovery, we applaud and support the work behind that decision. It takes incredible courage to recognize when something is taking on a toxic role in your life and then to do something about it. Listening to the reflections of our loved ones has led us to some of our own.

The act of pouring a drink or mixing a cocktail or a mocktail can be just as mindful as cooking. As we reflect on alcohol's role in a just kitchen, awareness and intention keep rising to the surface. Because of the people in our lives who have made different choices around drinking, we have begun to be more intentional about creating that mindful space, first as we decide what to drink, and then again as we pour or mix.

Because a just kitchen includes paying attention to the needs of those we gather with in the kitchen and at the table, we find an invitation to a mindful space preceded by a question: *Why am I drinking?* It's a question that honors answers such as celebrating the day's accomplishments, being in beautiful surroundings, or sharing good company. The answer that doesn't land in the just kitchen is "I need a drink." A just kitchen isn't one that dulls emotions.

To us, the Wendell Berry quote at the head of this section rings true. To take something celebratory and make it a means of escaping our lives doesn't honor the beauty of the thing nor the beauty of life. (While we are pointing to drinking here, it must be noted that we use this kind of escape with food too sometimes.) A good drink can draw us together, not push us into isolation. It should tune us in to the goodness of the world around us, not numb us to the point of missing that goodness.

Anthony Culbert, William Stevens, and Delvin Joyce, hosts of the *Black and Brown* podcast, are African American men who started getting serious about bourbon collecting and noticed there wasn't much representation of people of color in the industry. Their response was to start their show, which has given voice to Black and brown people and to women in the industry as together they explore the often-untold history of Black influences on distilling. The show doesn't shy away from questions about representation, says Anthony. "We always approach inclusion with [guests], because we have to ask them that tough question: Why are we missing?" They tackle these challenging issues without losing the vibe of three friends sharing a drink around a firepit.

Delvin described that vibe this way: "The fact that it's something that you put in your glass, that you have to take your time with it, and that you're probably around people that you really like and enjoy. But the bourbon, as it's going down, starts to loosen you up a little bit, and you're taking your time, and it's going to evoke some stories."

William added, "Bourbon is about storytelling. There's different styles and types of bourbon, and I think because of that, the complexity of the conversation mimics the complexity of the spirit."

Creating that atmosphere has allowed the three friends to build bridges in the bourbon community across racial and cultural lines. Anthony described an encounter with a distiller in Washington State that started out with uncertainty and ended with a great interaction and a quality barrel pick. "Ultimately, our goal is to bring people into our comfort zone. They're guests in our house, and we kind of make them feel at home, make them have some fun. We're going into their environment, they're coming to our environment, and we're trying to make each other feel comfortable about what's going on in the industry."

Whether bourbon around a firepit, a glass of wine while tending to the stove, or a beer as we keep company with the cook, a good drink can create the space for stories to be shared and life to be celebrated.

Don't Ruin Thanksgiving!
Derrick's Story

After a year of becoming fairly proficient with my new pellet smoker and smoking just about every meat imaginable, I decided that I needed a challenge, so I offered up the suggestion that I would make the Thanksgiving turkey in the smoker. My wife, knowing her husband's love for a slow, methodical process, had gifted the smoker to me. And since most things that can be smoked are best shared, we frequently had people over to enjoy more than just the aroma. I absolutely fell in love with my smoker.

I made a convincing argument for smoking the turkey and was given the green light. I researched how long to smoke the bird, how to season it, and, most importantly, how to keep the meat from being dry. (There's nothing worse than turkey with the consistency of sawdust!) I was fully prepared for everything—except the sudden pressure I felt around making the Thanksgiving *turkey.*

Now let's be honest: the turkey is nobody's favorite part of the Thanksgiving meal. Everyone has a side or a dessert that excites them far more. In my house, it is my wife's mac and cheese. Let's also acknowledge that at the time I made this decision, 75 percent of my children had already become vegetarian. They couldn't care less about what I was doing to the bird. All of that aside, I still felt this enormous weight about not screwing up the turkey. I felt it to such an extent that instead of buying one big turkey that would have led to weeks of turkey sandwiches, soup, and casserole, I bought two smaller birds and invited my neighbors over for a practice Thanksgiving dinner the week before.

The practice bird was a success, and my neighbors didn't mind being experimented on. But it dawned on me that evening that what had once been the

(continued)

joyful experience of making food for my friends and family had turned into a pressure-filled performance, despite the fact that the only one judging me was me.

Cooking for celebrations can easily take the celebration out of cooking—if we let it. When we allow our abilities in the kitchen to turn into a litmus test, we miss the opportunity to enjoy time with those we ultimately hope to show love to. At the end of the day, what matters are the people we get to share life's great moments with. And if they are the right people, anything can be forgiven. Even a dry turkey.

COOKING *FOR* CELEBRATION VS. COOKING *AS* CELEBRATION

Often what's required from us is a shift from cooking *for* celebration to cooking *as* celebration. Cooking for a celebration centers the event. Cooking as celebration centers the people and relationships being celebrated. Cooking for celebration happens on special occasions. Cooking as celebration can happen any day at any time.

Cooking as celebration can look like making someone's favorite meal or making a recipe from a family member who is no longer with us. Or sometimes it's as simple as knowing how your loved one likes a certain thing prepared. The importance is the emphasis on the person you are cooking for and your relationship to them.

There's a story Jesus tells in the Gospels, often referred to as the parable of the prodigal son. You likely know it: A son leaves home, taking his share of the family inheritance. His older brother stays home dutifully at his father's side, managing the affairs of the estate. The first son runs through his money on "riotous living," but when the parties end and his money is gone, he finds himself so hungry that he is lusting after the food he's feeding to pigs. He comes to his senses, leaves his last unfulfilling work, and returns home, humbled.

His father, who has obviously been waiting for him to return, sees him from afar and runs to meet him halfway. The wayward son tells his father that he is willing to come back as the hired help, but the father won't hear anything of it. He's going to have a party for his lost son who has returned. The father demands that the best fatted calf be killed and cooked for this feast. Despite all the pain this boy has caused himself and his father, his father finds reason to celebrate.

And because it's also a story of family dynamics (What celebratory feast isn't?), as the celebration is underway, the older brother returns from his work on the property and asks what's going on. When he's told his brother has returned and that his father has given the best of his animals to celebrate, the older brother confronts his father in anger, reminding him that when he asked for even a small goat to eat while hanging out with his friends, he was denied. No doubt feeling compassion for the hurt in his elder son's eyes, the father replies, "Your brother was, for all intents and purposes, dead. Now he's alive! That's worth celebrating! *He* is worth celebrating!"

Often, cooking for a celebration leaves us feeling like the older brother: unappreciated, overworked, and overlooked. Like the brother who never left, we can miss the importance of what is being celebrated.

We never find out what happens next in the story. Maybe the older brother storms off, now angry at his brother *and* his father. But we can imagine ourselves in the story and how we would hear Jesus's desire for his followers to live into the attitude taken on by the father: this brother, this son, is worth celebrating, and that celebration comes in the form of the best meal possible.

That shift from cooking for celebration to cooking as celebration helps us focus on the people around us and how we can show up in the kitchen in a whole and authentic way.

CELEBRATING OUR KITCHENS

Sometimes we celebrate events, occasions, or history. And sometimes our kitchens themselves can be celebrated. Nikki Cooley, who we met earlier, is co-manager of the Institute for Tribal Environmental Professionals' Tribes & Climate Change Program. She shared with us how she once dreamed of and longed for the kitchen she now has in the home she and her partner built together in Flagstaff, Arizona. They have an eight-year-old and a twelve-year-old, and there are always lots of kids and extended family coming over. "We still cook for everyone on the electric stove that my father-in-law gifted us after we got married. It's something I never thought I would own—I only thought that super-rich people in movies owned electric, glass stoves." So much of what fills her house now is her dream come true. "A lot of the stuff I have I did not grow up with—like electricity, my own shower, my own room. And my own kitchen." She explained that they had to share a lot of what they had on the reservation where she grew up. "It was a community area; wherever you went, it belonged to everyone. Everybody's in your space. You're in their space."

The kitchen she has now is still everybody's—at least everybody in the household—"but it's also something that I can call my own," Nikki said. "My husband built it specially to accommodate me. I love to cook, to bake, and to host people. It's not one of those kitchens you see in *Home and Garden* or on social media. There are dirty parts of it. There are dusty parts of it. You walk into that kitchen and you know that it's used and loved. And that everyone is welcomed there. There's a lot of love in that kitchen."

Like Nikki, you may have a long-desired kitchen, or you may be cooking in a kitchen that leaves much to be desired. Regardless of the circumstances, the practices of celebration and gratitude can be extended to the physical realities of our kitchens. Appreciating the little things in your kitchen can lead to it being a place you want to be. Noticing how the light comes in through the window in the morning or how the floor feels beneath your feet. Many of us bring in flowers, plants, brightly colored dish towels, and art to add beauty to our kitchens.

And we can't forget music! It's amazing how quickly your kitchen can turn into a dance party/karaoke bar with the right playlist. Especially if you are someone who doesn't particularly enjoy the act of cooking, but want to bring a celebratory, invitational feel to yourself and others, you might find a favorite album or a new album you haven't had a chance to listen to all the way through, and let the joy of music eclipse the drudgery you're feeling—or heighten the joy, if you already hold that in the kitchen.

What are the ways you can celebrate your own kitchen and make it a place that moves you to celebrate life?

Joy in Little Things
Anna's Story

Cooking with our toddler around when I'm in a hurry can be an exercise in frustration, but when I carve out the time to actually cook **with** *her, it can be a celebration. The other day, on my day off, we spent some time out in the garden. I would pull a carrot and she would take it and gleefully throw it in the basket. The onions went into the basket . . . and then back out onto the lawn . . . and then some made it back into the basket. All the while, I was trying to let go of my desire for order and to embrace her celebration of each vegetable going in and out.*

Having a toddler has helped me to find joy and celebration in the little things. I have never before in my life been reminded so often to look closely at a rotting tomato in the yard. My daughter's joy and interest in the little things, both literally and figuratively, has been an invitation to find joy and celebration in new ways—from celebrating the things I have always thought are awesome, like the hummingbird in the garden and the little purple eggplants popping out through the leaves, to things she's teaching me are exciting, like the noise of the blender or just how much fun it is to do dishes in the sink.

Later, after we brought the basket and ourselves into the kitchen and I slowed down enough to celebrate the preparation of this food with her, we washed the new potatoes we'd harvested together. I celebrated the beautiful deep purple tones of the potatoes, while she celebrated what you can do with a dribble of water and a sink full of vegetables. We played the handing-back-and-forth game again as I scrubbed the carrots from the garden, and she reminded me to taste-test them and make sure they were still delicious and fresh. Even her exclamations reminded me to celebrate. An excited "ahhhhh!!!" when I poured the potatoes into the water. Clapping and cheering after she successfully plopped a carrot in the sink. And excited squeals when the water got turned back on. My daughter reminds me that there is much to celebrate in the kitchen, even on an ordinary afternoon.

SHARING AS CELEBRATION

While we have poked at how social media can be intimidating as we see our friends' "perfect" dishes, both of us also experience sharing our cooking on social media as an opportunity to celebrate. When we cook that dinner using potatoes and onions that we grew in our own garden, or appreciate the intricate shapes on a head of Romanesco broccoli from the farmers' market, we want to share our excitement and joy.

There is something about sharing beauty with others, whether that's having folks around our tables or sharing virtually, that is nourishing and nurturing. Celebration can be a spiritual practice and part of our process of paying attention, as we keep our eyes out for that which is delicious and beautiful.

And celebration is linked closely to gratitude, as science tells us that consistently practicing gratitude actually rewires our brains. A study conducted in 2008 measured the brain activity of people who were thinking about and feeling gratitude. They found "that gratitude causes synchronized activation in multiple brain regions, and lights up parts of the brain's reward pathways and the hypothalamus. In short, gratitude can boost neurotransmitter serotonin and activate the brain stem to produce dopamine. Dopamine is our brain's pleasure chemical. The more we think positive, grateful thoughts, the healthier and happier we feel." When our kitchen is a place of celebration and gratitude, we may find ourselves seeking time in the kitchen as a place of joy and health and happiness.

Pastor Bruce Reyes-Chow has always found food presentation interesting. "When making teriyaki mashed potatoes," he said, "I would put them in the middle of a plate and try to make it look nice for whoever I was about to serve." For Bruce, even the simple act of plating food is an opportunity to make art, to feel joy, to be grateful for the food. The moment of presenting what we have just created is a wonderful opportunity to honor the work we've done and celebrate the act of sharing and eating.

As people who care about the well-being of humanity, we hope these stories and conversations can lead us collectively into a place of nourishing and celebrating greater joy and justice in our kitchens.

CLEANING UP

At the end of any cooking celebration, cleanup is a necessity. We wash the dishes for the sake of our future selves—for easy use the next time they are needed. Even in our cleanup, we can reimagine the power structures of our own kitchen as the one who cooks perhaps puts up their feet, maybe with a celebratory drink, as others pitch in, getting their hands into the dishpan. Or sometimes the cook wants to bring the day's events to a close, thinking through the gathering and the celebrations as guests have gone, and lingering in through the memory of the meal.

When we're paying attention to our kitchen as a place of reflection, we might find that washing the dishes isn't just a chore for what is past; it is the ritual for what is to come. Cleaning up prepares us for the next thing. As we clean up, we may find it is another opportunity to interact with each other.

Cleaning up engages us in the process of transformation as we watch our kitchen move from mess to order. Cleaning up provides us a chance to reflect on the meal, the people, and the process. Cleaning up also offers everyone the opportunity to participate with mutuality. And so, cleaning up in the kitchen is another place where community is built. In the cleanup time, there can even be healing as we think of cleaning as a metaphor and remember we can always start anew. Then there is the final celebration: the dishes are done! We live into the hope that the next day is on its way and the kitchen will be born again.

Food Instagram Accounts We Love

Adrian Miller – @soulfoodscholar

Eden Hagos – @edenthefoodie

America's Test Kitchen – @testkitchen

Museum of Food and Drink – @mofad

Fabiana Li – @food.anthro

Equity at the Table – @equityatthetable

Annie Levy – @kitchencounterculture

Kevin Mitchell – @chefscholar

Amy Halloran – @flourambassador

Chad Robertson – @tartinebaker

Collard Greens

Anthony "Da Plug" Culbert, from the Black and Brown *podcast*

Anthony made sure to tell us that these are not your momma's—nor her momma's—greens. He claims that these have been perfected after much trial and error and have turned collard green haters into true believers. You have been warned!

--------- **Recipe** ---------

INGREDIENTS

1–2 bunches collard greens
(You can use kale with the
collards if you choose. It's your
way, ya dig?!)
1 white onion diced
1 tablespoon red pepper flakes

4 garlic cloves minced
1 tablespoon Sambal Oelek chili
paste
1/4 cup honey or molasses
1 cup apple cider vinegar
2 cups chicken or vegetable stock

DIRECTIONS

1. Put a heavy-bottom pot or dutch oven over medium-high heat, and sauté the onion and red pepper flakes until onion is translucent, maybe 5–7 minutes. (I recommend sautéing in bacon grease. Coconut oil is also acceptable.) Add the garlic, and sauté an additional 30 seconds. Don't burn it—nobody likes it burned! After the aromatics are happy, add your sambal and sauté. The burn will let you know when it's ready.

2. At this point you can begin to add your collard greens and allow them to wilt. Keep adding until they are all in the pot. Drizzle in your honey, the chicken stock, and half of the apple cider vinegar. You can add the rest near the end of cooking as you taste. Salt and pepper to taste. After it comes to a boil, lower it to a simmer, cover, and cook for about 45 minutes.

3. Begin to test the greens for tenderness until they reach your desired level of doneness. Finish with apple cider vinegar to taste, and serve.

Cherry Bourbon Sour

Derrick Weston

Recipe

INGREDIENTS

6 fresh cherries (de-seeded)
1.5 ounce bourbon
3/4 ounce lemon juice

3/4 ounce simple syrup
1 egg white

DIRECTIONS

1. In a shaker or pint glass, muddle cherries, and add lemon, simple syrup, and then bourbon. Shake, add egg white, shake hard. Add ice to a rocks glass, and strain mixture into it. Garnish with an extra cherry. Replace bourbon with your favorite tea to make a Cherry Sour Mocktail.

Cooking Playlist

We asked our friends on social media to tell us what they like to listen to as they cook. Here is a sampling of the list that we crowdsourced:

1. "Paradise" by Sade

2. "Her Black Wings" by Danzig

3. "The Times They Are A-Changin'" by Bob Dylan

4. "Give Up the Funk" by Parliament

5. "Far Away" by Ingrid Michaelson

6. "Cruisin'" by Smokey Robinson

7. "World's Smallest Violin" by AJR

8. "Feelin' Good" by Nina Simone

9. "I Can Cook Too" by Patti Austin

10. "Red Beans and Rice" by Michael Franti and Spearhead

11. "Crowded Table" by The Highwaywomen

12. "Can I Kick It?" by A Tribe Called Quest

13. "Julep" by Punch Brothers

14. "Ain't No Mountain High Enough" by Marvin Gaye and Tammi Terrell

15. "My Favorite Things" by John Coltrane

LITURGY
Celebrate!

God who delights in all you have created,
We celebrate with you.

God who nourishes the seeds in the earth,
We celebrate with you.

God who is in the hands that cultivate,
We celebrate with you.

God who guides us in relationship,
We celebrate with you.

God who delights in the small and the large,
We celebrate with you.

God who sets time apart and who is in the ordinary,
We celebrate with you.

God who is in our kitchens with us,
We celebrate with you.

God who is holding all things,
We celebrate with you.

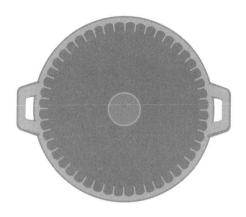

CHAPTER 10

THE KITCHEN AS A PLACE OF HOPE

Cooking, like gardening, is ultimately an act of hope. It is based on a belief that there is something worth living for that keeps us coming back to our kitchens and sustaining our bodies. In cooking and eating we find the strength to do the work of peace and justice in our communities. As we bring this book to a close, we want to revisit some of the ways the kitchen can become a space of dreaming for a hoped-for tomorrow and a conduit for a more faithful, more generous, and more just world. We also want to leave you with a couple of very practical things you can do to take steps toward the just kitchen you want to have in your home.

DOES MY KITCHEN COUNT?

You may be pondering questions such as these:

- What if I only cook once or twice a week and order out the rest of the time?
- What if my meal came from the prepared-foods section of the grocery store?
- What if everything in my kitchen is from a big-box store?
- Does my kitchen count as a "just kitchen"?

Many of us ask questions like these—questions about sourcing foods, accessibility, justice, and convenience when we're extremely busy. Hopefully, by this point in the book you'll have discovered that any kitchen can move toward being a just kitchen. There are no boxes to check. No forms to fill out. No declarations or signed contracts. What makes a kitchen just is the intention to bring your stories, values, and awareness to what you cook. It doesn't have to be every meal, every day. There will be lapses. There can be no perfectly just kitchen because there are no perfect acts of justice in this world. Every solution is incomplete, filled with trade-offs and compromises. Life is messy. People are complicated. All of our kitchens are messy and complicated—even the clean ones.

What Makes A Just Kitchen

There are no boxes to check. No forms to fill out. No declarations or statements of intent. What makes a kitchen just is bringing your stories, values, and awareness to what you cook. It won't be every meal, every day. There will be lapses and no kitchen is always just because there are no perfect acts of justice in the world. Still, even with kitchens that are messy and complicated—even the clean ones—we bring small and large actions of justice into our kitchens – and hold an abiding hope that justice, like a garden, will take root and grow.

Besides, as we mentioned in the opening chapter, there's a truth that has shaped every inch of this book: the system is rigged. We're overworked, overscheduled, and overextended. Perhaps there are solutions if we are willing to completely disengage from the politics and economics of our world, but that option is likely reserved for only the truly privileged and wealthy among us. Each of us has to find our own way to bring the things we care about most into the kitchen.

The just kitchen is one in which every effort is made to reduce the exploitation that takes place in the process of preparing food. That means not victimizing others based on race or gender, being conscientious of the environmental impacts of what we eat, and being mindful of the ways our cooking impacts our surrounding communities. It also means not abusing ourselves in a vain attempt to do all of this perfectly. Importantly, essentially, a just kitchen is a grace-filled kitchen.

LET'S TALK ABOUT COMPOST!

Most of this book has not been prescriptive, as we would rather present questions for consideration, which you—who know your kitchen and your life best—are better able to answer. We want this to be about exploration and finding your own way to a kitchen that is better for your family and the world.

We hold most things with an open hand and generous spirit, but we do have a few points we care deeply about. Among them: Folks, seriously, you should be composting!

If you've heard our podcast, you know we are passionate about compost. It's one of the easiest ways to give back to the world through your kitchen. Composting diverts organic matter from your trash can to some other container or bin where it can then break down and be used in your garden or lawn. This process of decomposition is often aided by worms. Composting simply lets nature do what nature does.

It's now easier than ever to compost. More and more cities and towns have compost pickup. There are many places where you can buy kitchen containers that will mitigate any smell. While numerous kinds of outdoor containers are for sale, if you're industrious enough, they are not hard to build. (Derrick built one, and admits he's better at the smoker than the carpentry tools.) You can even get compost worms delivered to your house if you're into that sort of thing. (We are! Anna may have even asked for, and received, worms for her birthday a few years ago.)

Some people live where there are restrictions on whether they can compost, but more and more areas are providing opportunities either to drop off compostable material or to have it picked up. If you can't compost at home, a quick online search can help you determine where you can deposit your compostables free of charge. It also can be a good way to connect with others who are striving to pay attention to food waste. We've been known to make friends around a compost pile and have them welcome us to bring our compostables over to theirs. Conversely, one of our compost bins quickly became the bin for the whole apartment building, as we converted others to the ease and power of compost.

While we hope this is a book you'll revisit and find new ways to incorporate into your daily life, we would consider it a success if the only thing you took away from these pages is that you *need to compost*.

Compost is also about as good a metaphor as you can find for the ebbs and flows of life, new life coming from death, or turning the messy parts of life into something beautiful. The things we think of as waste become food for another group of organisms, and the result is soil, the very foundation of life. Compost: rich in nutrients, rich in symbolism!

COMPOSTING HOPE

We started the book by talking about hope and are bringing it to a close with compost because composting reminds us that there is hope in the full cycle of things, even when it's messy. And on a practical note, composting completes the cycle in the kitchen and connects the kitchen to the farm, the table, and back again.

In terms of environmental justice, composting can play a big part in the puzzle of lowering emissions and lessening our impact on the climate crisis. Almost a quarter of what goes into landfills is food waste, and all of that food waste has to be transported by fuel-burning trucks to get there. Then, once it gets to the landfill, it isn't able to happily decompose. Instead, it's under pressure, almost as if it were in a plastic bag. Because of this, it can't naturally decompose and become soil, but instead emits more greenhouse gasses. But when you compost those same food scraps in your backyard, local community garden, or commercial composting, they actually help sequester carbon, as well as decomposing into nutrient-rich soil that can then be used to grow vibrant and disease-resistant plants.

Composting can also guide us to the spiritual practice of paying attention. Often when we start composting in earnest, we become appalled at how much food we were letting spoil in our refrigerator. And when we know the people who grew that food, our feelings about letting it rot heighten. The practice of composting may relieve some of our guilt, as at least the food will be reused and turn into soil. But it can also make us more mindful and can change our shopping and cooking habits. Paying attention to our compost may lead us to look in the fridge and ask, "What is about to spoil, and how can I cook that today?" We may be much more likely to throw together disparate leftovers or come up with some new creative dish because we don't want that broccoli to go bad.

In our interview with Connie McOsker, case manager at a family homeless shelter at Harbor Interfaith Services, along with her mother, Elia Tamburri, and

Connie's daughter, Nella, Nella lovingly teased Connie about the "food rescue" Connie has been doing for the past few years. Nella shared how it feels very connected to her childhood experience of her mom in their family kitchen— nothing ever went to waste. Connie laughingly recounted that if little Nella didn't like an ingredient, she'd hear, "You're gonna like it in the next meal, and you won't even know it's in there!"

"Leftovers took on this sort of everlasting quality," Nella jumped in, "where a little bit of a stew would go into the next meal, and some of that meal would go into the next."

Part of this recycling of food was a financial choice—with five children and college to pay for. But it wasn't just that. "There was always going to be some sort of creative ingredient in soups and salads," Nella remembered. "What do we have? How do we eat it and honor it? Food didn't wind up in the trash. Ever." Among the things composting reminds us of is the fact that there is value in everything created. Even what is often thought of as "trash" has something to contribute to the cycle.

HOPE IN THE COMPOST PILE

Compost also gives us a spiritual metaphor that we can lean into as we strive for just and hopeful kitchens. So often we can get weighed down by despair and hopelessness. The world is filled with brokenness and scraps and tired and wilted leftovers. We can see the exhaustion of people working for justice. We can get discouraged by the depths of division and discord. We can feel like throwing it all away and giving up. But compost reminds us that something is still ready to be used, and that we likely always have something to give that can be part of the next life cycle. For those who hold to faith traditions, we can sense that even our exhaustion and our wilted selves are precious to the Divine. God is ready to accept whatever we have to offer, individually and collectively, to nourish and nurture whatever is coming next for us.

Hope comes in the compost heap, and often not in the way we expect. Sometimes it's the random pumpkin plant from last year's jack-o-lantern seeds, or the connection made with a neighbor, which in turn starts to shift the culture in your town. Hope isn't what makes everything shiny and bright every day; it's something much more earthy and real than that. Hope is what gets us out of bed in the morning and helps us keep trying. Hope is what pushes us to ask for help, to believe there's another way, to try one more time. Hope is that little seed, deep beneath the earth, working its way toward the warmth of spring. Hope is continuing to show up in our cooking and our kitchens, even on the days when it feels hard or we feel discouraged, where we discover, somehow, some comfort and joy.

PRACTICE RESURRECTION

In the Christian tradition, the concept of resurrection is about something being made new, which is right in line with compost. The well-known phrase "practice resurrection" comes from a piece from farmer and author Wendell Berry and completes a beautiful list of mandates:

> *So, friends, every day do something*
> *that won't compute. Love the Lord.*
> *Love the world. . . .*
>
> . . . .
>
> *Ask the questions that have no answers.*
> *Invest in the millennium. Plant sequoias.*
>
> . . . .
>
> *Put your faith in the two inches of humus*
> *that will build under the trees*
> *every thousand years.*
>
> . . . .
>
> *Laugh.*
> *Laughter is immeasurable. Be joyful*
> *though you have considered all the facts.*
>
> . . . .
>
> *Practice resurrection.*

As we explore what it means to be seekers of love and justice in our kitchens, ending with the idea of a practice of resurrection seems fitting.

Because a practice, rather than an isolated snapshot, is something lasting, something transformative over time. Engaging in a practice permeates what we do and how we act; it changes our connection with the world around us. A practice is something that lives within a bigger cycle, a larger narrative, a life that is alive and aware of love and possibility. A practice keeps us steady in times of joy and in times of sorrow. The practices we enact in our kitchens are part of a much bigger story of creation and humanity, of this hope for a better world.

The story of Jesus shows us the practice of resurrection and the way of love. We see both throughout Jesus's life, from his birth in a lowly manger on the outskirts of town, to the way he reached out across boundaries, healing and teaching and eating with all sorts of people. Regular everyday people, preparing food and cooking and eating together in their kitchens.

We see Jesus's ministry being not one of power and control or of trying to impress or be in line with the forces of the day, but being about service and compassion, turning the world upside down for its own sake. Jesus was fully immersed in and among the messy reality of people's lives, being in human skin and encountering the struggles of humanity, even to the end. And Jesus was so relentless in his love that even after death, he practiced resurrection.

On the day before he died, he shared a meal with his closest friends and companions, where he took bread, broke it, and said, "Do this in remembrance of me," directing us, too, to keep coming around the table, sharing a meal together, and being knit together here in the world.

The next day, having been abused and, ultimately, left to die on the cross, even in moments of deepest abandonment and subjected to the worst of human violence, Jesus voiced love and forgiveness for his tormentors, before breathing his last.

But with divine love, death is never the final word. Divine love practices resurrection. In this larger story, love is always born anew, love persists through struggle, love overcomes pain, love is resurrected, love is transformed into life.

Now, practicing resurrection, walking in the story of love, and seeking justice and hope in our kitchens are never clear-cut or all-encompassing. We live in a complex and interconnected world. And even when we're taking steps toward a more just way of being, we still often don't really grasp how we are part of building something bigger, something even hopeful.

Rarely do we notice where new things are growing out of the dead and dying places in our lives and in the world. Rarely do we look for it in the mundane activities of our lives: washing vegetables, loading the dishwasher. We often only see what is right in front of us: what we've lost, what isn't working. Sometimes it's only in retrospect that we can turn and see where new life has come from. But whether or not we see it, God keeps practicing resurrection.

We all have our own stories. In this book, we shared bits of the stories of fellow inhabitants of kitchens across geography. Our hope is that in these stories you find an invitation to explore and tell your own stories and engage in practices that bring more justice and hope to your kitchen.

We find that hope in the promise of the cycles, of the seasons, of new life, drawing forth healing from that which is broken, abandoned, abused. Over breakfast, lunch, and dinner. When the kitchen is briefly clean and when it's a hot mess. Buried seeds bursting forth into bloom. Taking what is dead and raising it again, showing us that love always, always is being reborn among us.

The Divine Composter doesn't waste anything, but sees it all in the light of the cycle of life, death, and resurrection—a cycle that is led by love and justice's transformative power.

And we are not alone in this work. We are all mixed together in the divine compost heap, the potato peels and the leftover bread, where a new world is possible, where the way of the beloved community can be realized. It's coming, and it is here, in and among that which is changing and dying. We and our kitchens are part of it all.

What Gives Me Hope?
Anna's Story

Writing this book has taught me that I am not alone in hope. There is a community of people who are actively desiring and making choices toward another way. That gives me hope.

In the fall of 2022, Derrick hopped on a plane and flew from Maryland up to Massachusetts so we could have a few days of a writers retreat together. While Derrick and I have known each other from various conferences and our paths have crossed over the years, we had not seen each other in person since the fall of 2019. We had written the entirety of this very embodied and place-based book on cooking while being in different states and in different kitchens. And while we have exchanged a myriad of Zoom calls, texts, emails, and oh-so-many notes in the shared Google doc, we had not had the kind of conversations that can happen only while chopping carrots and picking the meat off a stewed chicken.

Standing in my kitchen I was struck by how the depth and textures of our conversations changed. And as we reflected, we both realized that we had been changed by this book and this writing process.

"I pay attention to my cooking in a different way," I shared. Derrick agreed.

Preparing the fresh sage and parsley we'd just picked from my garden, I was struck by what gives me hope. What gives me hope is that we can grow and learn and change. What gives me hope is that I, as someone who would have told you five years ago, or even fifteen years ago, that I cared about having a just kitchen, can tell you today that my kitchen and I have changed over the course of exploring the stories in this book. I find hope in the fact that there is no "arrival place" when it comes to living lives of justice. There is no final test or accomplishment when it comes to living faithfully toward the way of beloved community.

Instead, there is a continual invitation to take the next step, hear the next story, make the next change, slip backward, and have the grace to try again. That is practicing resurrection. And that gives me hope.

What Gives Me Hope?
Derrick's Story

In late 2019, my oldest daughter became a vegetarian. Months later, two of the other kids followed suit. These sudden-seeming changes in diet sparked a lot of conversations in our house about how we should treat animals, what is best for the environment, and what it means to be an ethical eater. My wife and I haven't joined our kids in their meatlessness (nor has our youngest son), but we have started eating less meat and now pursue better-raised and animal-honoring meat. Our cooking has changed because of our kids' convictions. Our children are thinking about ways they can make the world a better place. That, more than anything, gives me hope.

I am very aware of how far my real life is from my ideals on so many fronts, but especially in the kitchen. The truth of my kitchen is that there are fruit flies hovering around the tomatoes from my garden, there is an unused head of lettuce slowly rotting in the crisper, and family-sized containers of items from big-box stores make it hard to move around. The recycling bin is full of pizza boxes. The garbage has half of a kid's dinner that didn't make it into the compost despite my nagging.

What qualifies me to write about a just kitchen? It's been a surprise companion on this journey. A softer, quieter companion. I don't know if it is a new companion or one whose voice has been strengthened by the process of writing. It is a voice of attentiveness. It draws my attention to the people I am cooking for just as much as to the act of cooking. It occasionally snaps me out of my rush to get things on the table to appreciate the sound of boiling water, the smell of fresh herbs, and the feel of a knife against a cutting board.

It is a voice that draws my attention away from the fact that I didn't grow the lettuce myself and takes a second to pray for the hands that did. It is a voice that reminds me that "beef" is a cow, "pork" is a pig, and "poultry" is a chicken, and that all of those beings should be honored as they give their lives for ours.

It is a reminder that while billionaires own those stores that I am ashamed to have shopped in, the people working there and shopping there are doing what they can to put food on their own tables, and there is a dignity in that. It is a recognition that I am connected to the whole of creation in messy, complicated, beautiful, and surprising ways.

Early in this process, I described the book-in-progress to an acquaintance. Her eyes lit up as I shared that I hoped to break us out of seeing cooking as a chore. "Right," she responded. "It's not a chore, it's a ritual!" I agreed. And while rituals can be reduced to merely structural repetition, my hope is that we can see cooking as a ritual that honors the continuity of life. One thing dies that another might live. We are creatures, participating in the acts of creation. And yet we are the only creatures that cook. The lives that are preserved through cooking are ones with the opportunities to speak peace into the world, call out injustice, and make right what is wrong in our broken systems until they, too, become food for the life that will come after them.

My kids are part of the life that comes after me. With every meal I make them, I hope I am nurturing people who will speak truth to power. I hope I am fueling bodies that will stand up for the vulnerable. I hope that when they see me in the kitchen, they are invited into the delight that I feel in getting the opportunity to love them in such a tangible way.

I hope they see that my wife and I have tried our best to create a space of welcome and hospitality where all are afforded their due dignity. And I hope they will continue to be people who are uncomfortable with the world as it is and who will do the small, incremental things that make it better.

We end each episode of our podcast asking our guests, "What gives you hope? Not a hope that ignores the challenges of the world, but a hope that gives you the resilience to face those challenges." As we bring this book to a close, the question takes on a new shape. The question we're asking now is: *How can hope become one of the things that is produced in your kitchen?*

Mom's Sweet Potato Pie

Derrick Weston

--- **Recipe** ---

INGREDIENTS

3 sweet potatoes, cooked and peeled
(approx. 1 1/2 cups)
1 egg
1/2 cup raw sugar
1 teaspoon cinnamon

1 teaspoon nutmeg
1 teaspoon vanilla extract
1/2 cup melted butter
1/2 cup eggnog

DIRECTIONS

1. Mix ingredients in blender or food processor. Pour into uncooked pie crust (store-bought or your own). Bake at 350 degrees for 30–45 minutes (depending on the moisture of the sweet potatoes).

LITURGY
For Compost

Before the bowl flows over with onion peels
or gives home to the fruit flies,
Before the mold grows green,
I lift thee from the kitchen table
and carry you out to the heap of hot soil.
I lift you towards the heavens
before I release you.
You are an offering.
May you die well,
bless this dirt
and become life once more.
—Lydia Wylie-Kellermann

Acknowledgments

We are deeply grateful to the many guests that have come on the *Food and Faith Podcast* over the years, and particularly those who have shared the stories in this book. Thank you to Bruce Reyes-Chow, Isabel Ramirez-Burnett, Khadija Adams, Nikki Cooley, Anthony Culbert, Delvin Joyce, William Stephens, Maren Morgan, Jake Marquez, Ginny Messina, Dr. Christopher Carter, Hugh Hollowell, Justin Cox, Kelley Nikondeha, Kendall Vanderslice, Jason Chesnut, Lee Anderson, Nella McOsker, Connie McOsker, Elia Tamburri, Shani Mink, James Connolley, Holly Stallcup, Karen Mann, Nora Woofenden, and Harshita Bhargava. We have learned and grown through the generosity of your stories, and we look forward to them being out there in the world.

We offer thanks to those who have nurtured the work of the *Food and Faith Podcast* since the beginning. Especially our founding co-host Sam Chamelin, and early supporters and conversation partners Jana Carter, Fred Bahnson, Nurya Love Parish, Heber Brown, Jason Chesnut, and Kendall Vanderslice.

We are incredibly grateful for the whole team at Broadleaf. Particularly our Lil Copan, who has brilliantly nurtured this book since it's inception. And we thank the editorial, design, and marketing teams, and thanks to Rachel Reyes who has kept us all on track. We are grateful to Skye Kerr Levy, Ian Woofenden, Garrett Andrew, and Akirah Wyatt for their support, insights, and feedback along the way.

Anna

I give thanks to my parents and grandparents for forming my first memories in the kitchen and showing me that food and cooking were important and valued parts of life.

I give thanks to my siblings, with whom I share a love of creating meals and taking what we learned in childhood and making it our own.

I give thanks for chosen families in my adult years, who invited me into their kitchens and offered me places to belong.

I give thanks to the faith communities who have shown me how cooking in community is an act of worship and hope.

I give thanks to Derrick, co-author, collaborator, and friend, for being on this creative journey as a team.

I give thanks for my spouse, who more than shares the cooking in our household and who nourishes us in so many ways.

And I give thanks for our daughter, Jarena, who is teaching me daily and inspires continued commitment to the life of faith, hope, justice, and love.

Derrick

First off, I'm grateful to Anna for thinking of me when this idea was presented to her. I could not have imagined then where that first phone call would lead us both. I'm blessed to have someone in my life who makes my ideas better! Thank you, Friend!

To everyone that said, "That sounds like a cool book" at any point in the writing process, thank you! You kept me going!

Thanks to Chris Holmes for the use of the Peace House where this book was outlined and much of the brainstorming happened. Thanks to Alex Askew and the Mindful Eating for the Beloved Community program as well as "Protest Kitchen" authors Virginia Messina and Carol Adams. Your influences helped to shape the content and tone of this book.

I'm grateful for the Death in Garden discord community, several of whom are featured in this book. Thanks for the insightful conversations and your deep desire to make the world a healthier place.

To Lindsey, for helping me build the infrastructure for emotions, for the language of cooking as a ritual, and for being a steadying presence for most of the last decade.

Thanks to my neighbors Alex, Lisa, Joe, and Rachel for all the dinners you've made for me and the few I've gotten to make for you. Thank you for modeling hospitality and generosity!

To Dawn and Diego, thank you for sharing your love of food and for simply being awesome friends!

Jason, thank you for being a great creative partner and for being someone I can talk to when my brain isn't my friend. Go Niners!

To the Ruthers, thanks for being friends that feel like family!

To Nate and April . . . there's not enough space here to express my love and gratitude for you both. Thanks for keeping me alive and not giving up on me!

To RJ, Freda, Rachelle, and Ronald... God picked a strange time to bring you into my life but I'm so grateful that you (and your families) are here!

To Mom, Dad, Damen, Cybil, and Chrissy, thanks for loving me even when I am terrible at being a son and a brother.

To Maggie, Thomas, Gus, and Sophia . . . I love being your dad. I hope this makes you proud.

And last, but certainly not least to Shannon, thank you for being my partner in all things. Your love sustains me. I promise that I'll mention you earlier in the next book!

Notes

All liturgies, unless otherwise noted, by Anna Woofenden.
All recipes used by permission of contributors.

Chapter 1

More information on the 2019 Pew Research poll can be found here: Katherine
   Schaeffer, "Among U.S. Couples, Women Do More Cooking and Grocery
   Shopping Than Men," *Pew Research Center*, September 24, 2019, https://www.
   pewresearch.org/fact-tank/2019/09/24/among-u-s-couples-women-do-more-
   cooking-and-grocery-shopping-than-men/

Chapter 2

Excerpt from Gary Nabhan, *Jesus for Farmers and Fishers: Justice for All Those
   Marginalized by Our Food System* (Minneapolis: Broadleaf Books, 2021),
   114–115. Used by permission.

Recipe from Christopher Carter, *The Spirit of Soul Food: Race, Faith, and Food Justice*
   (Urbana: University of Illinois Press, 2021), 20–21. Used by permission.

Chapter 3

The five practical suggestions for preparing our kitchen come from Cambria Bold,
   "5 Things You Should Do before You Turn On a Burner," *Kitchn*, April 30, 2015,
   https://www.thekitchn.com/5-things-to-do-before-you-turn-on-the-burner-
   life-in-the-kitchen-218777.

Chapter 4

"There Is Enough," by Kerri Meyer, https://www.musicthatmakescommunity.
   org/there_is_enough. Used by permission. Kerri has given faith
   communities permission to sing and share the song without copyright
   restrictions. You can find the sheet music here: https://drive.google.com/file/
   d/1JNUxOsP8feFUST7gwEY8FSChFR-4iEfW/view

Black bean soup recipe by The Moosewood Collective from *Moosewood Restaurant Cooks at Home: Fast and Easy Recipes for Any Day* (New York: Simon and Schuster, 1994), 23–24.

Chapter 5

Mindfulness breath prayer for washing dishes, by Christine Valters Paintner, from *Breath Prayer: An Ancient Practice for the Everyday Sacred* (Minneapolis: Broadleaf Books, 2021), 76. Used by permission.

Chapter 7

The quote "the beloved community" is from Martin Luther King, Jr., *The Christian Century* magazine, July 13, 1966.

The quote "This is what God's kingdom is like . . ." is from Rachel Held Evans, *Searching for Sunday: Loving, Leaving, and Finding the Church* (Thomas Nelson, 2015), 148.

Lentil Soup and No-Knead Bread recipes, from Alissa Wilkinson, *Salty: Lessons on Eating, Drinking, and Living from Revolutionary Women* (Minneapolis: Broadleaf, 2022). Used by permission with minor adaptation.

Chapter 8

The quote from Heber Brown III is from Amy Frykholm's interview with him, found here: "The Black Church Food Security Network Aims to Heal the Land and Heal the Soul," *Christian Century*, November 10, 2020, https://www. christiancentury.org/article/interview/black-church-food-security-network-aims-heal-land-and-heal-soul.

Chapter 9

Quote on fasting from Rabbi Irwin Kula and Vanessa L. Ochs, "A Meditation on Fasting," *Bread, Body, Spirit: Finding the Sacred in Food*, ed. Alice Peck (Woodstock, VT: SkyLight Paths, 2008), 116.

Quote on scientific findings about gratitude is from "Gratitude and the Brain: What Is Happening?," *Brain Balance*, https://www.brainbalancecenters.com/blog/gratitude-and-the-brain-what-is-happening.

Chapter 10

The "Practice resurrection" quote is from Wendell Berry, "Manifesto: Mad Farmer Liberation Front" from New Collected Poems. Copyright © 2010 by Wendell Berry. Reprinted with the permission of The Permissions Company, LLC on behalf of Counterpoint Press, counterpointpress.com.

"For Compost," by Lydia Wylie-Kellerman, originally published in the booklet *Dirty Prayers* by *Geez* magazine. Used by kind permission of Lydia Wylie-Kellerman.

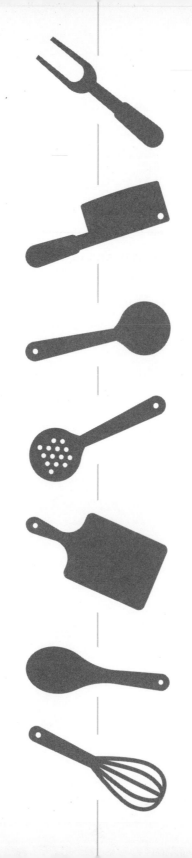